A GUIDE TO BIRD FINDING IN KANSAS AND WESTERN MISSOURI

UNIVERSITY PRESS OF KANSAS

A GUIDE TO

Bird Finding in Kansas and Western Missouri

JOHN L. ZIMMERMAN AND

SEBASTIAN T. PATTI

ILLUSTRATED BY ROBERT M. MENGEL

Published by the University Press of Kansas (Lawrence,
Kansas 66049), which was organized by the Kansas Board
of Regents and is operated and funded by Emporia State
University, Fort Hays State University, Kansas State
University, Pittsburg State University, the University of
Kansas, and Wichita State University

Library of Congress Cataloging-in-Publication Data
Zimmerman, John L., 1933–
    A guide to bird finding in Kansas and western Missouri /
John L. Zimmerman and Sebastian T. Patti; illustrated by
Robert M. Mengel.
        p. cm.
    Bibliography: p.
    Includes index.
    ISBN 0-7006-0365-4. ISBN 0-7006-0366-2 (pbk.)
    1. Bird watching—Kansas—Guide-books. 2. Bird
watching—Missouri—Guide-books.   I. Patti, Sebastian
T.   II. Mengel, Robert Morrow, 1921–   .   III. Title.
QL684.K2Z55 1988
598'.07'234781—dc19   87-34655

Printed in the United States of America
10 9 8 7 6 5 4 3 2

CONTENTS

ILLUSTRATIONS

ACKNOWLEDGMENTS

A great number of bird enthusiasts have helped us in a variety of ways to develop this book, from just a casual mention of a possible site to careful evaluation of preliminary tour write-ups. We would especially like to thank Dan Bowen, Roger Boyd, Tom Cannon, Karen Cartlidge, Mary Clark, Mel Cooksey, Steve Crawford, Tom Flowers, Bob Gress, Larry Herbert, Allen Jahn, Earl McHugh, Mike Mueller, Jay Newton, David Rintoul, Stan Roth, Richard Rucker, Joe Schafer, Jean Schulenberg, Marvin Schwilling, Scott Seltman, Tom Shane, Max Thompson, Byron Walker, Gerald Wiens, and Eugene C. Williams.

We are grateful to Paula A. Strafuss, cartographer, who not only produced the maps with dispatch but also made suggestions to improve their utility.

We also thank Jan Posey for her efforts in the preparation of the manuscript and Dana Custer and Lou Ann Claassen for their assistance in this endeavor.

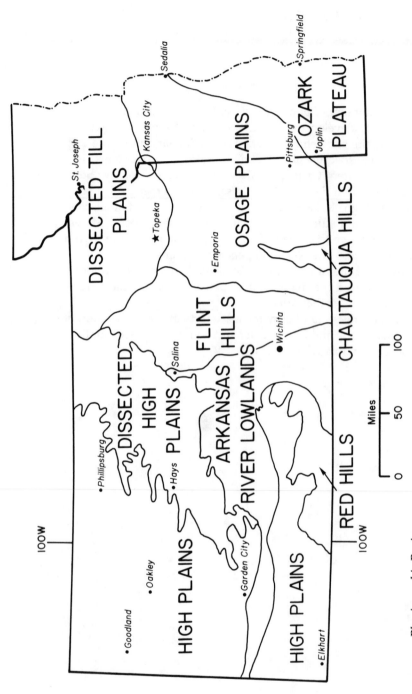

MAP 1. *Physiographic Regions*

INTRODUCTION

You cannot see the Front Range from the western border of Kansas, but the effects of the Rocky Mountains modify the biota of lands east to the Mississippi River and beyond. A knowledgeable observer traveling west from Indiana might discern subtle shifts in the composition of forests and in the plants growing along railroad rights-of-way, but from western Missouri to the far edge of Kansas change becomes obvious. Biotic transition is the theme when moving west into the deepening rain shadow of the Rocky Mountains; it is the phenomenon that makes bird finding in western Missouri and Kansas an adventure in expecting the unexpected.

A May morning in the Ozark Plateau of southwestern Missouri is not too different from a morning in southern Ohio. Carolina Chickadees are bringing food to their nestlings in an old woodpecker hole; Acadian Flycatchers sing from perches along forested canyons cut by streams cascading over limestone ledges. Mixed-species flocks of wood warblers replenish at the expense of caterpillars from the forest canopy the fat stores consumed in last night's migratory flight. Yet one might see a Scissor-tailed Flycatcher or a Swainson's Hawk over an upland "bald" of bluestem prairie. In the Flint Hills on that May morning the birding experience is different. Summer Tanagers and Louisiana Waterthrushes of the eastern forest still defend territories in the galleries of hackberry and bur oak that parallel the lower stream courses, but in the upland tall-grass prairie the doleful "old-mul-doon" and treble cackles of the Greater Prairie-chicken are detectable above the sound of the wind while the parabolic song-flight of the Upland Sandpiper interrupts the horizon. In the plains beyond the hundredth meridian you are indeed "out west." The sky is punctuated by the displays of Lark Buntings and Cassin's Sparrows, and along the Cimarron River migrant Western Wood-pewees and MacGillivray's Warblers feed in the shrubs and cottonwoods. But it is not too surprising if an American Redstart or even a Blackburnian Warbler appears with a flock of Audubon's and Orange-crowns; and although most orioles are Bullock's, a few are Baltimores, and others are somewhere in between.

From Branson MO in the southeast to St. Francis KS about five hundred miles to the northwest, the avifauna changes markedly. Over two dozen species reach the western limit of their continental range across the span of this diagonal. Some of these birds are closely allied to the eastern deciduous forest. Wood Duck, Red-bellied Woodpecker, Tufted Titmouse, Wood Thrush, Kentucky Warbler, and Scarlet Tanager are species that disappear as the forest itself disappears in the face of diminishing rainfall. Others are grassland birds dependent upon the more mesic prairie—Sedge Wren, Eastern Meadowlark, and Henslow's Sparrow dropping out as tall-grass prairie is replaced by mixed prairie and the short-grass plains. A smaller number of breeding species, such as the Common Poorwill, Say's Phoebe, Chihuahuan Raven, and Rock Wren, are typical of the arid southwestern United States and occur no farther east than Kansas. There are four species of southwestern xeric steppe that reach their northern breeding limit—Lesser Prairie-chicken, Scaled Quail, Greater Roadrunner, and Cassin's Sparrow. Several species of the southeastern United States reach the northern extent of their breeding range as well, for example, Carolina Chickadee, Chuck-will's-widow, and Painted Bunting. And for a few species, Kansas and western Missouri are on the southern fringe of their breeding distribution. This group, however, is ecologically diverse—aquatic birds like the Redhead and Black Tern, the grassland-adapted Bobolink, and the Cedar Waxwing and Black-capped Chickadee of the eastern deciduous forest.

Major ecological associations of species come together in the midcontinent, generating spatial diversity in their interdigitations. Of the environmental variables that determine ecological patterns, the balance between rainfall and evaporation is primary in affecting the biotic characteristics of this region. In western Missouri annual rainfall averages about 40 inches, but it decreases to less than 20 inches per year at the Colorado border. In the eastern half of this region, rainfall exceeds evaporation; in the western two-thirds of Kansas water is in deficit. Across this moisture gradient oak-hickory forest is successively replaced by tall-grass prairie, which in turn is replaced by mixed prairie and finally the short grass of the high plains. These longitudinal bands of dominant vegetation are superimposed upon a topography that ranges in elevation from around 600 feet above sea level in western Missouri to over 4,000 feet near the Colorado border. The interaction of the broad ecological patterns and the physiography of the region leads to a mosaic of ecological communities in which more than 400 species of birds can be found. This book is your guide across this mosaic.

Major Biotic Communities and Their Birds

It is not possible to locate all the places in the region where bird finding would be rewarding. Indeed, we have purposely selected sites where public access is unrestricted and natural areas are available to the public with prior permission of managers or owners. We believe an ecological overview of the region will enhance your appreciation of the avian diversity as well as increase your chances of finding the birds you seek. To paraphrase the ecologist G. Evelyn Hutchinson, your enjoyment of the play of life will be increased by your understanding of the ecological theater in which it takes place.

Eastern Deciduous Forest Biome

The deciduous forest covers most of the eastern half of the United States and forms what ecologists classify as a biome, a relatively uniform type of vegetation that occurs across a broad geographic area. The eastern deciduous forest biome in western Missouri and Kansas is represented by three distinct communities—Ozark forest, oak-hickory forest, and riparian (floodplain) forest.

OZARK FOREST. The northern edge of the Ozark Plateau cuts northeasterly from southeastern Kansas, just west of Joplin MO, to the Missouri River north of Sedalia. The Ozark forest covers most of this physiographic region, and two-thirds of all Missouri's forested lands occur in the Ozarks. The dominant species are bitternut hickory (*Carya cordiformis*), shagbark hickory (*C. ovata*), white oak (*Quercus alba*), and Shumard's oak (*Q. shumardii*). In addition to these, sugar maple (*Acer saccharum*), white ash (*Fraxinus americana*), deciduous holly (*Ilex decidua*), black walnut (*Juglans nigra*), and wild black cherry (*Prunus serotina*) are important species in the forest. The breeding bird population in this forest type, particularly in southwestern Missouri and southeastern Kansas, is characterized by Red-shouldered Hawk, Whip-poor-will, Pileated Woodpecker, Acadian Flycatcher, Carolina Chickadee, Carolina Wren, Wood Thrush, Yellow-throated

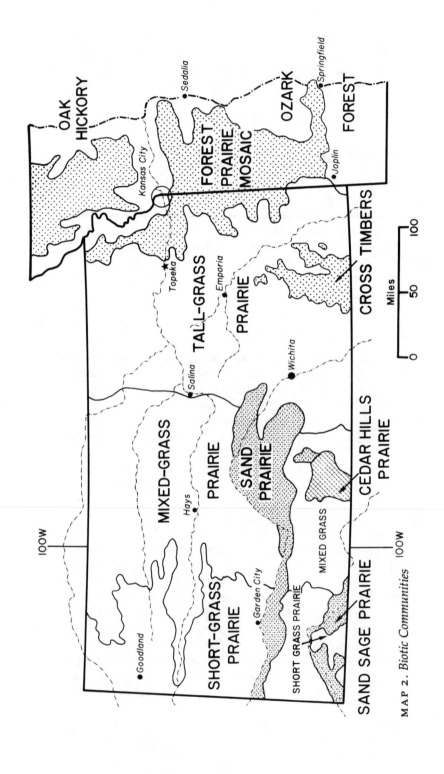

MAP 2. *Biotic Communities*

OAK HICKORY

FOREST PRAIRIE MOSAIC

OZARK FOREST

Sedalia

Springfield

Kansas City

Joplin

TALL-GRASS PRAIRIE

Topeka

Emporia

CROSS TIMBERS

Miles

100

50

0

MIXED-GRASS PRAIRIE

Salina

Wichita

SAND PRAIRIE

CEDAR HILLS PRAIRIE

Hays

100W

MIXED GRASS

SHORT-GRASS PRAIRIE

Garden City

SHORT GRASS PRAIRIE

SAND SAGE PRAIRIE

100W

Goodland

Vireo, Scarlet Tanager, and a variety of wood warblers, such as Northern Parula, Yellow-throated, Cerulean, Black-and-white, Worm-eating, Ovenbird, and Hooded.

OAK-HICKORY FOREST. A little over a million years ago the first of the glaciers that would later move southward across the continent developed and barely reached the northern edge of this region. The second major glacial period, 780,000 to 670,000 years ago, affected the topography of this area, leaving behind remnants in the glacial till plains of northern Missouri and northeastern Kansas. The Big Blue River, which joins the Kansas River at Manhattan and in turn becomes confluent with the Missouri River at Kansas City, forms the approximate boundary of glaciated terrain. Lands to the west of the Big Blue and south of the Kansas and Missouri have never been glaciated.

The oak-hickory forest occurs on the uplands of the glacial till plains of Missouri, bounded on the west by the Missouri River upstream from Kansas City. To the south the oak-hickory forest merges with the Ozark forest, and like the Ozark forest it is dominated by bitternut hickory, shagbark hickory, and white oak. But the more southerly Shumard's oak is replaced by red oak (Q. borealis) and black oak (Q. velutina) among the codominants. The breeding bird population is similar to that of the Ozarks except that the Black-capped Chickadee replaces the Carolina Chickadee, and other southern species like the Yellow-throated Warbler are absent.

RIPARIAN (FLOODPLAIN) FORESTS. In the bottomlands of the Missouri River and its tributaries and west along the Kansas River and its branches as well as along the Marais des Cygnes, Neosho, Osage, and Spring rivers, the eastern deciduous forest is a community of species dominated by hackberry (Celtis occidentalis), cottonwood (Populus deltoides), and American elm (Ulmus americana) with green ash (F. pennsylvanica), black walnut, sycamore (Plantanus occidentalis), buckeye (Aesculus glabra), and bur oak (Q. macrocarpa) as notable components. To the west in the Flint Hills Upland, the riparian forest is confined to the first couple of terraces in the floodplain, forming a narrow "gallery" along the water courses. Farther west, trees are still present in the floodplain, but they become progressively more widely scattered with increasing longitude, allowing grasses to replace the more shade tolerant herbaceous plants on the forest floor and forming a riparian woodland rather than a forest. Most species of the eastern deciduous forest also disappear; thus, the riparian woodland in western Kansas is largely one species, cottonwood.

In the eastern part of the region the riparian forest has a greater avian variety than the upland oak-hickory forest. Many species of the Ozark forest occur, like Acadian Flycatcher, Prothonotary Warbler, and (rarely) Hooded Warbler, finding suitable nesting habitat in the moister floodplain. But to the west the riparian community becomes less diverse by the loss of true forest species. The Louisiana Waterthrush and Northern Parula, for example, are near their western limit in the Flint Hills. Tufted Titmouse, Wood Thrush, and Rose-breasted Grosbeak extend a little farther west, but then they, too, drop out of the community. As the riparian forest becomes riparian woodland there is an enrichment with the increase in edge; here Northern (Bullock's) Oriole, Orchard Oriole, Warbling Vireo, Yellow Warbler, House Wren, Black-billed Magpie, and Western Kingbird become conspicuous members of the avifauna.

Forest-Prairie Mosaic

The demarcation between the eastern deciduous forest and the grassland biome is not abrupt. Prairies form "balds" on exposed dolomitic bedrock in the uplands of the Ozark Plateau, but the predominant vegetation is forest. Away from the rivers and streams and their riparian vegetation on the till plains of northern Missouri and extreme eastern Kansas and across the eastern half of the Osage Plains, there is a vast intermingling of these two biomes. Ecologists call this merging an ecotone, with forest and prairie forming a patchwork of habitats. Throughout much of the area, however, forests have been reduced, and cultivated crops have replaced the prairie. Nevertheless, this region provides good birding because of intermingling habitats and abundant edge. From a single vantage point, for example, the song of the Wood Thrush can be heard from the interior of a forest island while despotic Dickcissels contest for territorial space in adjacent fields and Bell's Vireos scold in the thickets.

The cross-timbers area of the Chautauqua Hills in southeastern Kansas forms another mosaic of prairie and forest, in this case stands of blackjack (*Q. marilandica*) and post (*Q. stellata*) oak on the ridges with intervening prairie and cultivated fields in the lowlands. The bird community in this area is not distinct from other comparable areas in the forest-prairie mosaic except for the presence of more southern species like the Painted Bunting.

Islands of upland deciduous forest become scarce west of the ninety-sixth meridian, but not until the Flint Hills Upland does true or tall-grass prairie dominate the landscape. Even here the lowlands with their deeper alluvial soils have been converted into agricultural production of row crops, but the shallow soils and alternating beds of shale and limestone have discouraged the plow in the uplands. Here the last major remnant of the great tall-grass prairie that once stretched east to the Wabash River, across Indiana, and into the uplands of Ohio remains close to its primeval state. Cattle have replaced the bison and elk as large grazers, and the wolf and bear are gone, but because of good range management practices the prairie has remained otherwise ecologically intact, as evidenced by the abundance of the Greater Prairie-chicken throughout the Flint Hills.

Four species of grasses that grow and flower during the warm season of the year characterize the tall-grass prairie—big bluestem (*Andropogon gerardii*), little bluestem (*A. scoparius*), indian grass (*Sorghastrum nutans*), and switchgrass (*Panicum virgatum*). (In good rainfall years big bluestem can grow to be taller than eight feet.) Also, abundant herbaceous forbs provide striking seasonal aspects to the prairie. However, the bird community is not especially diverse. Just four species comprise two-thirds of the population—Dickcissel, Brown-headed Cowbird, Eastern Meadowlark, and Grasshopper Sparrow. Mourning Dove, Upland Sandpiper, Common Nighthawk, and Greater Prairie-chicken compose most of the remaining third. In the clumps of dogwood (*Cornus drummondii*) along lower limestone benches, Bell's Vireo, Brown Thrasher, and Bewick's Wren breed, and on the higher rock outcrops Common Poorwills nest. During late summer in swales of prairie cordgrass (*Spartina pectinata*) along stream drainages, Sedge Wrens arrive to nest.

In the Arkansas River Lowlands windblown sand dunes have been stabilized by prairie vegetation, and sandreed (*Calamovilfa longifolia*) occurring along with big and little bluestem forms the sand prairie. The region provides an interesting mix of eastern, western, and southern bird species. The breeding bird survey route conducted annually near St. John in Stafford County KS regularly records Burrowing Owls and Say's Phoebe of the west, Northern Cardinals and Red-bellied Woodpeckers of the east, and the more southern Greater Roadrunner.

The sand dunes along the Cimarron River in southwestern

Kansas have been vegetated by little bluestem, sandreed, sand bluestem (*Andropogon hallii*), and sandhill sage (*Artemisia filifolia*). The bird community of the sandsage prairie is decidedly flavored by affinities with the arid southwestern United States: Lesser Prairie-chicken, Scaled Quail, and Cassin's Sparrow are common, but Ladder-backed Woodpecker, Curve-billed Thrasher, and Cassin's Kingbird can be occasionally discovered.

In the tall-grass prairie sideoats grama (*Bouteloua curtipendula*) is present, but in the Dissected High Plains west of the ninety-eighth meridian sideoats grama and blue grama (*B. gracilis*) obtain codominance with big bluestem and little bluestem. This is the mixed-grass prairie. Although a distinct plant community, its avian community is not especially different from that of the tall-grass prairie; for example, Henslow's Sparrows are not present, but another eastern species, the Red-eyed Vireo, still can be found in associated riparian woodland. The Dickcissel becomes less abundant, replaced in oldfield communities by the Lark Bunting; and Horned Larks become frequent in the more openly structured habitat.

In the Red Hills along the southern border of Kansas between the Arkansas River Lowlands and the High Plains, the mixed-grass prairie occurs with an overstory of red cedar (*Juniperus virginiana*). Historically this Cedar Hills prairie provided suitable habitat for the Black-capped Vireo, but there have been no recent nesting records of this species in Kansas. This region, however, supports a high nesting population of the Mississippi Kite.

The short-grass prairie of the High Plains region begins in Kansas and extends westward to the base of the Rocky Mountains. It is dominated by blue grama and buffalo grass (*Buchloë dactyloides*), and as in all grasslands, the bird community is simple. Horned Lark, Grasshopper Sparrow, Mourning Dove, and Western Meadowlark are the abundant species. Ferruginous Hawk, Long-billed Curlew, and formerly the Mountain Plover, although less abundant, are uniquely characteristic of this community. In recent years the area covered by short-grass prairie has been rapidly decreased in extent by widespread implementation of irrigation for cultivated crops.

Aquatic Communities

Lakes are characteristic of a geologically young landscape. Given enough time the erosive activity of water converts all watersheds into streams. Since much of western Missouri and Kansas is unglaciated, time has been on the side of the streams; therefore, natural lakes are rare, occurring usually quite ephemerally as ox-bows cut off during floods on the major rivers. The building of numerous reservoirs, particularly in the last thirty years, how-ever, has greatly increased surface waters in the region and pro-vided habitat for migratory and wintering waterfowl. But few of these impoundments have developed extensive freshwater marshes.

Of particular interest are the saline lakes and salt marshes dominated by saltgrass (*Distichlis stricta*). Two sites in the sand prairie habitat of the Arkansas River Lowlands, Cheyenne Bot-toms, and Quivira National Wildlife Refuge are outstanding wet-lands that attract large numbers of migrant and nesting water-fowl, shorebirds, and marsh dwellers. As a result of increasing competition for water from agronomic uses, the dependability of water for fall migration and occasionally for breeding has been drastically reduced in recent years.

Seasons

Kansas and western Missouri lie within the zone of interaction between the major air masses that affect the climate of North America. In summer warm, moist, unstable tropical maritime air flowing north from the Gulf of Mexico dominates the weather, occasionally being pushed aside in western Kansas by the hot, dry, unstable tropical continental air from the desert Southwest. These air masses are frequently displaced by polar maritime air that is cool and stable, having lost its moisture in crossing the Rocky Mountains. Thus, the mean monthly temperatures during June, July, and August range from the middle 70s to 80 (F) de-grees in western Missouri and eastern Kansas, but the tempera-tures are a couple of degrees cooler in the High Plains of the west. The relative humidity can often be high in the east, but the air becomes progressively drier towards the west. More than 70 percent of the annual rainfall occurs within the growing season, and June is the rainiest month. July is the hottest month with average daily maximum temperatures of 92 to 94 degrees and average minimums of 62 to 68 degrees. The average number of days when temperatures are 100 degrees or greater ranges from ten to twenty per year.

Fall is characterized by the increasing frequency of fronts that bring colder, drier polar continental air into the area. Mean monthly temperatures from September to November range from 41 to 68 degrees in the east and from 44 to 70 degrees in the west. Rainfall decreases from the summer high, and the days are quite pleasant with winter held at bay until after Thanksgiving. Although most passerine migration is concentrated in the forested habitats east of the tall-grass prairie, isolated stands of riparian woodlands in the west are often magnets for a variety of migrants. All the lakes and reservoirs within the area attract waterfowl and other waterbirds, sometimes in spectacular concentrations. July and August can often be quite dry so suitable habitat for shorebirds is limited, yet certain sites are traditional stopovers for the fall passage (see Great Bend KS and Stafford KS).

Mean monthly winter temperatures range from 30 to 34 degrees with only ten to fifteen days of snow cover in the south and thirty to thirty-five days in the north. Average maximum daily temperatures in January, the coldest month, range from 36 to 46 degrees, and average daily minimums range from 14 to 24 degrees. Winters are dry; only 3 percent of the annual precipitation falls in January. There are some characteristic patterns in the winter bird populations. Because western montane species move out on the plains, Red-shafted Flickers can be found east to the Missouri state line, Townsend's Solitaires are regular in the thick stands of junipers in the Flint Hills, and Mountain Bluebirds can be expected across the mixed-grass prairie. Huge flocks of Horned Larks and longspurs occur west of the Flint Hills, usually accompanied by a few Prairie Falcons. As has come to be expected throughout the Great Plains, numerous reservoirs attract wintering concentrations of Bald Eagles; and as long as the waters remain open, there is a satisfying variety of waterfowl as well.

The harbinger of spring is the first flock of migrant Northern Pintails. Another sign is the increase in the wind velocity, highest during the months of March and April. Mean monthly temperatures from March through May range from 44 to 65 degrees in the east and from 42 to 62 degrees in the western High Plains. Spring is also the time of the most severe weather as the warm, moisture-laden tropical maritime air mass again moves north to confront the colder polar air masses that have governed the winter.

Figure 1. SEASONAL OCCURRENCE AND RELATIVE ABUNDANCES OF REGIONAL BIRDS

All of the very rare species that are included in the checklist in the appendix have been excluded from this figure, since they are not to be expected. On the other extreme, House Sparrow, European Starling, and Rock Dove have also been excluded. For each species, the bar represents the occurrence of the species in the areas where it is to be expected. Thus the bar for Scaled Quail designates its status in the sandsage and short-grass prairie areas. The bar for Yellow-throated Warbler designates its status in the Ozark forest. No bar represents an "average" across the area covered by this guide. The four categories used for relative abundance are defined and symbolized as follows:

• • • •RARE. Very few records, not to be expected.

-- -- --OCCASIONAL. Irregular during the season indicated; or if regular, irregular in its annual frequency of occurrence.

————— UNCOMMON. Present during the seasons indicated at low densities. Appropriate habitats must be searched.

—————COMMON. Present in moderate densities during the seasons indicated and can be expected in appropriate habitats.

▬▬▬ABUNDANT. Occurs at high densities, a very noticeable species in appropriate habitats.

	MAR	APR	MAY	JUN	JUL	AUG	SEP	OCT	NOV	DEC	JAN	FEB
COMMON LOON												
PIED-BILLED GREBE												
HORNED GREBE												
EARED GREBE												
WESTERN GREBE												
WHITE PELICAN												
DOUBLE-CRESTED CORMORANT												
OLIVACEOUS CORMORANT												
AMERICAN BITTERN												
LEAST BITTERN												
GREAT BLUE HERON												
GREAT EGRET												
SNOWY EGRET												
LITTLE BLUE HERON												
TRICOLORED HERON												
CATTLE EGRET												
GREEN-BACKED HERON												
BLACK-CROWNED NIGHT-HERON												
YELLOW-CROWNED NIGHT-HERON												
WHITE-FACED IBIS												
TUNDRA SWAN												
GREATER WHITE-FRONTED GOOSE												
SNOW GOOSE												
ROSS' GOOSE												
CANADA GOOSE												
WOOD DUCK												
GREEN-WINGED TEAL												
AMERICAN BLACK DUCK												
MALLARD												
NORTHERN PINTAIL												
BLUE-WINGED TEAL												
CINNAMON TEAL												
NORTHERN SHOVELER												
GADWALL												
AMERICAN WIGEON												
CANVASBACK												
REDHEAD												
RING-NECKED DUCK												
GREATER SCAUP												
LESSER SCAUP												
OLDSQUAW												
SURF SCOTER												
WHITE-WINGED SCOTER												
COMMON GOLDENEYE												
BUFFLEHEAD												
HOODED MERGANSER												
COMMON MERGANSER												
RED-BREASTED MERGANSER												
RUDDY DUCK												
TURKEY VULTURE												
MISSISSIPPI KITE												
OSPREY												
BALD EAGLE												
NORTHERN HARRIER												
SHARP-SHINNED HAWK												
COOPER'S HAWK												
NORTHERN GOSHAWK												

	MAR	APR	MAY	JUN	JUL	AUG	SEP	OCT	NOV	DEC	JAN	FEB
RED-SHOULDERED HAWK												
BROAD-WINGED HAWK												
SWAINSON'S HAWK												
RED-TAILED HAWK												
FERRUGINOUS HAWK												
ROUGH-LEGGED HAWK												
GOLDEN EAGLE												
AMERICAN KESTREL												
MERLIN												
PEREGRINE FALCON												
PRAIRIE FALCON												
RING-NECKED PHEASANT												
GREATER PRAIRIE-CHICKEN												
LESSER PRAIRIE-CHICKEN												
WILD TURKEY												
NORTHERN BOBWHITE												
SCALED QUAIL												
YELLOW RAIL												
BLACK RAIL												
KING RAIL												
VIRGINIA RAIL												
SORA												
COMMON MOORHEN												
AMERICAN COOT												
SANDHILL CRANE												
WHOOPING CRANE												
BLACK-BELLIED PLOVER												
LESSER GOLDEN PLOVER												
SNOWY PLOVER												
SEMIPALMATED PLOVER												
PIPING PLOVER												
KILLDEER												
BLACK-NECKED STILT												
AMERICAN AVOCET												
GREATER YELLOWLEGS												
LESSER YELLOWLEGS												
SOLITARY SANDPIPER												
WILLET												
SPOTTED SANDPIPER												
UPLAND SANDPIPER												
WHIMBREL												
LONG-BILLED CURLEW												
HUDSONIAN GODWIT												
MARBLED GODWIT												
RUDDY TURNSTONE												
RED KNOT												
SANDERLING												
SEMIPALMATED SANDPIPER												
WESTERN SANDPIPER												
LEAST SANDPIPER												
WHITE-RUMPED SANDPIPER												
BAIRD'S SANDPIPER												
PECTORAL SANDPIPER												
DUNLIN												
STILT SANDPIPER												
BUFF-BREASTED SANDPIPER												
SHORT-BILLED DOWITCHER												

	MAR	APR	MAY	JUN	JUL	AUG	SEP	OCT	NOV	DEC	JAN	FEB
LONG-BILLED DOWITCHER	━	━	-	--	--	--	--					
COMMON SNIPE	━	━							--	--		
AMERICAN WOODCOCK	━											
WILSON'S PHALAROPE		━	━	--	--	--						
RED-NECKED PHALAROPE			•				--	--				
RED PHALAROPE							•	•	•			
FRANKLIN'S GULL		━										
BONAPARTE'S GULL	-	--	-				--	--				
RING-BILLED GULL	━	━										
HERRING GULL	━	--					--					
GLAUCOUS GULL									•	•	•	•
BLACK-LEGGED KITTIWAKE							•	•				
SABINE'S GULL							•	•				
CASPIAN TERN		━		—			--					
COMMON TERN		--	--					--	-			
FORSTER'S TERN		━	-	--	--	--		━				
LEAST TERN			-	--	--	--	-					
BLACK TERN			-	--	--	--	-					
MOURNING DOVE	━	━	━	━	━	━	━	━	━			
INCA DOVE	•								•	•	•	
COMMON GROUND DOVE									•			
BLACK-BILLED CUCKOO												
YELLOW-BILLED CUCKOO		━	━	━	━	━						
GREATER ROADRUNNER		--	--	--	--	--	--	--	--			
COMMON BARN-OWL	━	━	━	━	━	━	━	━	━	━	━	━
EASTERN SCREECH-OWL	━	━	━	━	━	━	━	━	━	━	━	━
GREAT HORNED OWL	━	━	━	━	━	━	━	━	━	━	━	━
SNOWY OWL										•	•	
BURROWING OWL	━	—										
BARRED OWL	━	━	━	━	━	━	━	━	━	━	━	━
LONG-EARED OWL	--	--	--	--	--	--	--	--	--			
SHORT-EARED OWL		--	--	--	--	--	--	--				
NORTHERN SAW-WHET OWL									•	•	•	•
COMMON NIGHTHAWK												
COMMON POORWILL		━	━	━	━	━	━					
CHUCK-WILL'S-WIDOW		━	━	━	━	━						
WHIP-POOR-WILL		━	━	━	━	━	━					
CHIMNEY SWIFT		━	━	━	━	━	━					
RUBY-THROATED HUMMINGBIRD		━	━	━	━	━	━					
BELTED KINGFISHER	━	━	━	━	━	━	━	━	━	━	━	━
RED-HEADED WOODPECKER	━	━	━	━	━	━	━	━	━	━	━	━
RED-BELLIED WOODPECKER	━	━	━	━	━	━	━	━	━	━	━	━
YELLOW-BELLIED SAPSUCKER	--	--						━	-	--	--	--
LADDER-BACKED WOODPECKER	━	━	━	━	━	━	━	━	━	━	━	━
DOWNY WOODPECKER	━	━	━	━	━	━	━	━	━	━	━	━
HAIRY WOODPECKER	━	━	━	━	━	━	━	━	━	━	━	━
NORTHERN FLICKER	━	━	━	━	━	━	━	━	━	━	━	━
PILEATED WOODPECKER	━	━	━	━	━	━	━	━	━	━	━	━
OLIVE-SIDED FLYCATCHER		━	━				━					
WESTERN WOOD-PEWEE				--	--	--	-					
EASTERN WOOD-PEWEE		━	━	━	━	━	━					
YELLOW-BELLIED FLYCATCHER		-					--					
ACADIAN FLYCATCHER												
ALDER FLYCATCHER			--			-	--					
WILLOW FLYCATCHER		--	•	•		-	--					
LEAST FLYCATCHER		━	━			━	━					
EASTERN PHOEBE												

MAR APR MAY JUN JUL AUG SEP OCT NOV DEC JAN FEB

SAY'S PHOEBE ....
ASH-THROATED FLYCATCHER........
GREAT CRESTED FLYCATCHER ....
CASSIN'S KINGBIRD ....
WESTERN KINGBIRD................
EASTERN KINGBIRD ....
SCISSOR-TAILED FLYCATCHER ....
HORNED LARK.....................
PURPLE MARTIN ....
TREE SWALLOW....................
N. ROUGH-WINGED SWALLOW.......
BANK SWALLOW ....
CLIFF SWALLOW ....
BARN SWALLOW ....
STELLER'S JAY.....................
BLUE JAY ....
SCRUB JAY........................
PINYON JAY ....
CLARK'S NUTCRACKER.............
BLACK-BILLED MAGPIE ....
AMERICAN CROW.................
CHIHUAHUAN RAVEN..............
BLACK-CAPPED CHICKADEE ....
CAROLINA CHICKADEE.............
MOUNTAIN CHICKADEE ....
TUFTED TITMOUSE ....
RED-BREASTED NUTHATCH.........
WHITE-BREASTED NUTHATCH ....
PYGMY NUTHATCH ....
BROWN CREEPER..................
ROCK WREN ....
CAROLINA WREN ....
BEWICK'S WREN ....
HOUSE WREN.....................
WINTER WREN....................
SEDGE WREN ....
MARSH WREN ....
GOLDEN-CROWNED KINGLET........
RUBY-CROWNED KINGLET ....
BLUE-GRAY GNATCATCHER.........
EASTERN BLUEBIRD ....
MOUNTAIN BLUEBIRD ....
TOWNSEND'S SOLITAIRE............
VEERY ....
GRAY-CHEEKED THRUSH ....
SWAINSON'S THRUSH ....
HERMIT THRUSH...................
WOOD THRUSH....................
AMERICAN ROBIN.................
GRAY CATBIRD....................
NORTHERN MOCKINGBIRD ....
SAGE THRASHER...................
BROWN THRASHER.................
CURVE-BILLED THRASHER ....
WATER PIPIT ....
SPRAGUE'S PIPIT ....
BOHEMIAN WAXWING..............

Introduction

	MAR	APR	MAY	JUN	JUL	AUG	SEP	OCT	NOV	DEC	JAN	FEB
CEDAR WAXWING												
NORTHERN SHRIKE												
LOGGERHEAD SHRIKE												
WHITE-EYED VIREO												
BELL'S VIREO												
SOLITARY VIREO												
YELLOW-THROATED VIREO												
WARBLING VIREO												
PHILADELPHIA VIREO												
RED-EYED VIREO												
BLUE-WINGED WARBLER												
GOLDEN-WINGED WARBLER												
TENNESSEE WARBLER												
ORANGE-CROWNED WARBLER												
NASHVILLE WARBLER												
NORTHERN PARULA												
YELLOW WARBLER												
CHESTNUT-SIDED WARBLER												
MAGNOLIA WARBLER												
CAPE MAY WARBLER												
BLACK-THROATED BLUE WARBLER												
YELLOW-RUMPED WARBLER												
BLACK-THROATED GRAY WARBLER												
TOWNSEND'S WARBLER												
BLACK-THR. GREEN WARBLER												
BLACKBURNIAN WARBLER												
YELLOW-THROATED WARBLER												
PINE WARBLER												
PRAIRIE WARBLER												
PALM WARBLER												
BAY-BREASTED WARBLER												
BLACKPOLL WARBLER												
CERULEAN WARBLER												
BLACK-AND-WHITE WARBLER												
AMERICAN REDSTART												
PROTHONOTARY WARBLER												
WORM-EATING WARBLER												
OVENBIRD												
NORTHERN WATERTHRUSH												
LOUISIANA WATERTHRUSH												
KENTUCKY WARBLER												
CONNECTICUT WARBLER												
MOURNING WARBLER												
MACGILLIVRAY'S WARBLER												
COMMON YELLOWTHROAT												
HOODED WARBLER												
WILSON'S WARBLER												
CANADA WARBLER												
YELLOW-BREASTED CHAT												
SUMMER TANAGER												
SCARLET TANAGER												
WESTERN TANAGER												
NORTHERN CARDINAL												
ROSE-BREASTED GROSBEAK												
BLACK-HEADED GROSBEAK												
BLUE GROSBEAK												
LAZULI BUNTING												

	MAR	APR	MAY	JUN	JUL	AUG	SEP	OCT	NOV	DEC	JAN	FEB
INDIGO BUNTING												
PAINTED BUNTING												
DICKCISSEL												
GREEN-TAILED TOWHEE												
RUFOUS-SIDED TOWHEE												
BROWN TOWHEE												
BACHMAN'S SPARROW												
CASSIN'S SPARROW												
RUFOUS-CROWNED SPARROW												
AMERICAN TREE SPARROW												
CHIPPING SPARROW												
CLAY-COLORED SPARROW												
BREWER'S SPARROW												
FIELD SPARROW												
VESPER SPARROW												
LARK SPARROW												
SAGE SPARROW												
LARK BUNTING												
SAVANNAH SPARROW												
BAIRD'S SPARROW												
GRASSHOPPER SPARROW												
HENSLOW'S SPARROW												
LE CONTE'S SPARROW												
SHARP-TAILED SPARROW												
FOX SPARROW												
SONG SPARROW												
LINCOLN'S SPARROW												
SWAMP SPARROW												
WHITE-THROATED SPARROW												
WHITE-CROWNED SPARROW												
HARRIS' SPARROW												
DARK-EYED JUNCO												
McCOWN'S LONGSPUR												
LAPLAND LONGSPUR												
SMITH'S LONGSPUR												
CHESTNUT-COLLARED LONGSPUR												
SNOW BUNTING												
BOBOLINK												
RED-WINGED BLACKBIRD												
EASTERN MEADOWLARK												
WESTERN MEADOWLARK												
YELLOW-HEADED BLACKBIRD												
RUSTY BLACKBIRD												
BREWER'S BLACKBIRD												
GREAT-TAILED GRACKLE												
COMMON GRACKLE												
BROWN-HEADED COWBIRD												
ORCHARD ORIOLE												
NORTHERN ORIOLE												
PINE GROSBEAK												
PURPLE FINCH												
HOUSE FINCH												
RED CROSSBILL												
WHITE-WINGED CROSSBILL												
COMMON REDPOLL												
PINE SISKIN												
AMERICAN GOLDFINCH												
EVENING GROSBEAK												

OZARK FOREST

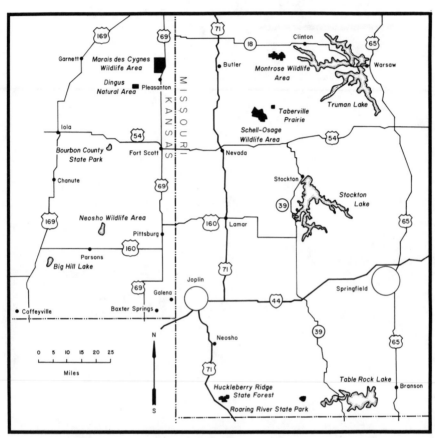

MAP 3. *Ozark Forest and Southern Forest-Prairie Mosaic*

BRANSON, MISSOURI

The White River flows north out of the Ozarks in Arkansas and has been dammed just west of Branson on U.S. 65 in southern Missouri to form Table Rock Lake. The Ozark forest surrounding this 20-mile-long lake within the Mark Twain National Forest offers the visiting birder abundant opportunities to sample the birdlife of the area.

Start your tour in Branson and go south out of town across the White River. At the junction of this highway with Lake Road 165-45, turn right and go west for just a short distance to reach the School of the Ozarks campus. This is one of the more reliable places in the area for finding the Greater Roadrunner, although this species has become somewhat irregular in recent years in southwestern Missouri.

Return to U.S. 65 and continue south for about a mile and turn right on M165. Drive west for about 6 miles to reach the entrance to Table Rock State Park and follow the road to the dam and visitors' center. From this unobstructed view of the lake you can expect some waterfowl at all times of the year, although large rafts of ducks will be present only during fall, winter, and spring. You should take the nature trail at the visitors' center and walk the woods in the state park. You will see several species of woodpeckers, including Pileated Woodpecker, as well as Carolina Wren, Carolina Chickadee, Tufted Titmouse, and White-breasted Nuthatch. In the winter, you should find both species of kinglets working the woods with the resident parids, Eastern Bluebirds, and Hermit Thrushes. In appropriate habitat the sparrow flocks will be quite diverse with Field, Fox, Song, Lincoln's, and White-throated Sparrows among the expected species.

Leave the state park the way you came in, but at Baird Mountain turn right on M265 to reach U.S. 65 in about 2.5 miles. Turn right on U.S. 65 and continue south for a little more than 2.5 miles and turn right (west) on M86. In 6.6 miles you reach a junction with County Road JJ. If you turn right here and drive north, you reach the lake at Coombs Ferry Access, which provides an additional vantage point to scan the next bend in the lake west of the state park. At 6.9 miles on M86 from Route JJ you reach the junction with M13. Turn right here and proceed north towards Kimberling City. The bridge across the lake just south of Kimberling City provides another place to stop and search the surface for waterfowl. This is also a good place to see Red-shouldered Hawks during any season.

Return to M86 and continue west through Ozark forest broken occasionally by cedar glades. If you stop at some of these glades in the breeding season, you should hear White-eyed Vireo, Prairie Warbler, Yellow-breasted Chat, Field and Grasshopper Sparrows, Blue Grosbeak, Indigo Bunting, and perhaps Painted Bunting. If you are very lucky, you might hear the lovely song of the Bachman's Sparrow, an uncommon breeder in this part of the state.

At 8.9 miles from M13 you come to the intersection with M39 in the town of Carr Lane. If you continue west on M86 from this intersection you can reach Roaring River State Park (see Cassville MO). But now, turn north on M39, go a little more than 3 miles, and turn right (east) on County Road H. After about 1.5 miles, take the road to Pilot Knob Mountain, where there is a U.S. Forest Service fire tower. The forest around the tower should have breeding Great Crested Flycatcher, Eastern Wood-pewee, Wood Thrush, Black-and-white Warbler, Kentucky Warbler, and Ovenbird. You might also hear the sharp "putt-putt" of Wild Turkey. If you visit these woods at dusk, you might hear Great Horned and Barred Owls, Eastern Screech-owl, Whip-poor-will, and Chuck-will's-widow. If you continue east on Route H after leaving Pilot Knob Mountain, you reach the lake at Big Indian Access, again providing the opportunity to search for waterbirds.

Return to M39 and turn right to continue north. In 5.2 miles you cross the western portion of Table Rock Lake. County Road YY goes east just north of the bridge and takes you to Campbell Point, providing another view of the lake. Continue north on M39 to Hill City and turn right on Lake Road 39-1, which soon parallels the southern boundary of the Piney Creek Wilderness Area. At the first intersection, about 3.5 miles from M39, turn left and follow this road north down to Piney Creek. This is a delightfully pristine area, and during the breeding season you can find Yellow-throated and Red-eyed Vireos, Northern Parula, Worm-eating Warbler, Prothonotary Warbler, Cerulean Warbler, Yellow-throated Warbler, Kentucky Warbler, and Lousiana Waterthrush.

Retrace your route back to Hill City and turn right on M39. In just a short distance you come to the intersection with M76. If you turn right here, you cross the James River arm of Table Rock

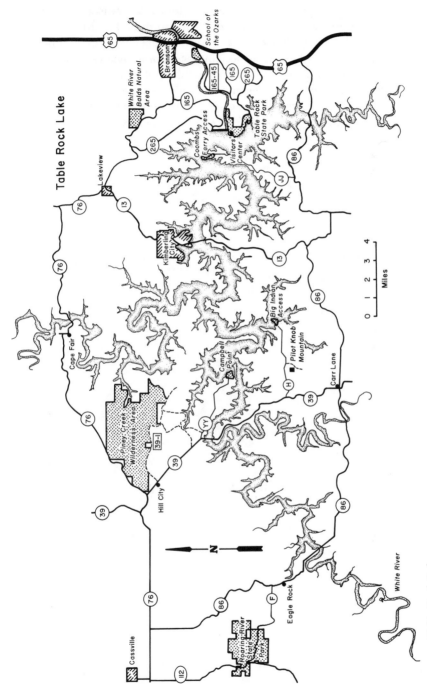

Table Rock Lake

White River Balds Natural Area

School of the Ozarks

Branson

Table Rock State Park

Visitors Center

Coombs Ferry Access

Lakeview

Kimberling City

Cape Fair

Piney Creek Wilderness Area

Hill City

Campbell Point

Big Indian Access

Pilot Knob Mountain

Carr Lane

N

Cassville

Roaring River State Park

Eagle Rock

White River

0 1 2 3 4
Miles

MAP 4. Table Rock Lake

Lake near Cape Fair and eventually return to Branson. About 4 miles northwest of Branson you come to the White River Balds Natural Area within the Ruth and Paul Henning State Forest. This 362-acre site is not especially noted for its avian species, but it is ecologically interesting as a natural prairie glade formed on dolomite with smoke tree and Ashe juniper, prairie wildflowers, and collared lizards. If you choose not to return to Branson, you can continue west on M76 to M112 and then south to Roaring River State Park.

CASSVILLE, MISSOURI

If you can only visit one location that typifies the Ozark forest
community, go to Roaring River State Park and the adjacent unit
of the Mark Twain National Forest. Although winter birding is
satisfactory, the best opportunities for birds are from the end of
April through September. The steep, forested hills dissected by
rocky ravines cut by swift, clear streams are the Ozarks; and
without a doubt, this is the best place to see warblers. If you're
tired of nothing but orange-crowns and butter-butts and think a
good warbler day is when you see a couple of Black-throated
Greens and a Blackburnian, come here. Fifteen species of warblers are known to nest in the park, and during migration flocks
of these and other species can be observed. As a result, a good
morning in May or September can easily produce a warbler list
exceeding twenty-five species! It is always best to come as soon
after sunrise as possible, especially in the spring, since the warbler chorus is at its peak and the "people traffic" at its lowest.

To reach the park, travel south for about 7 miles from Cassville
on M112. As you descend the steep hill just before reaching the
park boundary, you will understand why this park has developed a reputation as a "warbler wonderland." At the bottom of
the hill, bear left. This road crosses the stream twice; each time
you should stop and listen for Eastern Phoebes. Then park your
car near the fish hatchery tanks and walk up the road that runs
past the visitors' cabins, crossing the stream once again. This
road then enters the woods and parallels the stream for about
0.5 mile. During May and June you should find Blue-winged,
Yellow-throated, and Cerulean Warblers as well as Louisiana
Waterthrushes and Yellow-breasted Chats close to the trail.

Return to the intersection at the bottom of the hill that you
came to soon after entering the park, and take Route F toward
Eagle Rock. About 100 yards beyond the bridge, take the right
fork in the road marked "Dead End," and continue for about 0.6
mile to the end of the road where you can park. Walk down to
the river and take the trail that runs downstream for about a
quarter mile. Watch for Yellow-throated Warblers in the sycamores, Prairie Warblers in the cedars, and Black-and-white and
Cerulean Warblers in any deciduous trees. You should also find

The loud song of the Kentucky Warbler draws your attention, but it will take patience to find him sitting motionless in an understory tree of the forest. Birds feeding on late summer's ripening poison ivy provide a lesser challenge.

American Redstarts and Louisiana Waterthrushes. Retrace your steps, drive back to the fork in the road, and continue toward Eagle Rock. After about a mile, you come to the trailhead parking area for the "Wild Area Trail." This is a 3.5-mile loop trail that wanders up through forested hillsides to the crest of the tallest ridge in the area, and you should attempt this trek only if you are in reasonably good physical condition. It will take a careful birder several hours to complete, but you should find Worm-eating Warblers, Ovenbirds, and Yellow-throated Vireos here as well as other species characteristic of the drier slopes and uplands.

When you get back in your car and continue toward Eagle Rock on Route F, you will note several private roads leading down to Roaring River. Be sure to get permission if you choose to drive down any of these roads, but this effort will be well worth your time. Possible species along this stretch of the river include Northern Parula, Prothonotary and Yellow Warblers, Common Yellowthroat, and White-eyed Vireo quite literally "all over the place." And always watch overhead for Red-shouldered Hawks. Route F eventually intersects M86 where you should turn left (north). This road ascends rapidly through Mark Twain National Forest, reaching M76 after about 8 miles. As you drive this stretch of highway you will see many pull-offs at forest trails. It would be worthwhile to stop at any of these associated with logged areas now replaced by second growth in hopes of finding Hooded, Prairie, and Blue-winged Warblers as well as Yellow-breasted Chats and White-eyed Vireos. If you come upon a stand of pine, stop and listen for the dry trills of Pine Warblers.

If you get to M76, return to Roaring River State Park by turning left on M76 and going 3 miles to M112 where you should turn left (south) and continue for 5 miles until the junction with Route F. Or if it's shorter, retrace your route to the junction of M112 and Route F. From this intersection, continue south on M112 towards Seligman, going up the steep hill. At 2.3 miles past the motel at the top of the hill National Forest Scenic Drive Road 197 branches east toward Eagle Rock. This road is 8 miles long and provides many stops where you can find good numbers of migrant warblers in May and September. At 1.5 miles east of the junction of this forest service road and M112, National Forest Scenic Drive 198 forks off. This is a rough road that dead-ends in Butler Hollow after just 0.8 mile. Indeed, if you'd rather walk it, do so; you should find Hooded, Worm-eating, and Kentucky Warblers in the "holler" as well as Eastern Wood-pewees and Acadian Flycatchers. Also watch for Painted Buntings in the open areas at the end of the road. As you drive the remaining 6.5 miles to Eagle Rock on Forest Road 197, stop at the scenic overlooks and listen for Cerulean, Kentucky, and Hooded Warblers on the steep hillsides. In areas of cedar, listen for Prairie Warblers.

___

The Ozark Plateau cuts the corner of southeastern Kansas between Baxter Springs and Galena in Cherokee County and provides the only region of the state where you can expect the birds of the Ozark forest community. Because of this, the best time to visit the area is in May and June, during spring migration and early summer when the breeding species are actively advertising their territories and migrants of a more eastern continental distribution, like many of the wood warblers, will be passing through. A full day in the field during early May should produce a list of well over a hundred species.

Start your tour in Galena, 12 miles west of Joplin MO on U.S. 66. About 1.5 miles from the Kansas–Missouri border in the center of town, U.S. 66 joins K26. Go south from this intersection on K26, and in about 1 mile you will reach Schermerhorn Park. The Mississippian rocks that outcrop in this Galena city park along Shoal Creek are the oldest surface rocks in Kansas, and the large oaks in the uplands and especially the large sycamores along the creek provide excellent habitat for forest species. The Red-shouldered Hawk can be found in this area. Woodpeckers are most numerous; all resident species, including the Pileated Woodpecker, are present. Acadian Flycatchers occur during the breeding season along with White-breasted Nuthatch, Carolina Chickadee, Tufted Titmouse, Carolina Wren, both species of tanagers, Blue-gray Gnatcatcher, Great Crested Flycatcher, and Yellow-throated Vireo. As you walk through the riparian forest along Shoal Creek, listen for the Louisiana Waterthrush. The park is the only confirmed nesting location in Kansas for the Yellow-throated Warbler; other breeding warblers include Cerulean and Kentucky. A visit to the park at dusk could produce Eastern Screech-owl, Barred Owl, and Great Horned Owl. In the breeding season, Whip-poor-will and Chuck-will's-widow join these night singers.

Leave Schermerhorn Park and continue south on K26 to its intersection with U.S. 166. Turn right (west) here and continue for about 4.5 miles to the Spring River, just east of Baxter Springs. Riverside Park is on both the east and west sides of the river on the south side of the highway, and Kiwanis Park is west of the river on the north side of the highway. You should explore these sites for forest species, and the nearby sewage lagoons provide possibilities for waterfowl, gulls and terns, and waders, depending upon the season. From the river continue west on u.s. 166 through Baxter Springs to reach the cemetery on the north side of the highway, about 2.5 miles from the junction with u.s. 66 in Baxter Springs. Watch for resident Great Horned Owls and Northern Mockingbirds. During the summer expect Blue Grosbeaks and Bewick's Wrens in the surrounding open areas and second growth.

PINEVILLE, MISSOURI

Approximately 36 miles south of Joplin MO on u.s. 71 you reach Pineville in the most southwesterly of Missouri counties. Just 3 miles east of Pineville is Huckleberry Ridge State Forest, a mix of old and second growth with stands of pine and climax Ozark forest. It is best to visit this area during periods of spring and fall migration when warblers and other migrants are often present in large numbers. The summer months are just about as good, too, since this area provides habitats for the breeding birds typical of the Ozark forest region—Summer and Scarlet Tanagers, Great Crested Flycatcher, and Ovenbird in deciduous stands, Pine Warbler in pines, and Blue-winged and Prairie Warblers and Yellow-breasted Chat in cut-over and second-growth stands.

Going south on u.s. 71, turn left (east) on McDonald County Route k just south of Pineville. Highway k literally snakes its way through the forest, so exercise some care when driving this road at dawn and dusk as well as at night. Park in the primitive campground 4.5 miles east of Pineville and walk some of the trails. Both tanagers can be expected, and listen carefully for Black-and-white Warblers mixed with the more resounding song of Ovenbirds. In addition to the expected warblers in second-growth areas, you will also see Wild Turkeys if you are lucky. In the early spring, late fall, and winter, these woods have large feeding flocks that include both species of kinglets, Brown Creepers, and Carolina Chickadees.

Route k eventually intersects m90 where you can turn right (west) to return to u.s. 71, but if you've hit a good warbler flight it might be worthwhile to turn left (east) and do some birding at Roaring River State Park (see Cassville MO).

SPRINGFIELD, MISSOURI

This major city in southwestern Missouri offers several important birding locales. While April and May are probably the most productive months to visit because of the spring waterfowl and passerine migration, bird-watching opportunities occur throughout the year, and October has the extra advantage of the display of fall foliage for which the Ozarks are famous.

The best introduction to the birds of this area is at Lake Springfield in the southeastern corner of the city. Take U.S. 60/BUS. RT 65 (Glenstone Avenue) south to the interchange with U.S. 65, then go south on U.S. 65 to exit within less than a mile at Evans Road. The lake lies just to the west. Both puddle ducks and diving ducks can be expected here, as well as Double-crested Cormorant and probably a Common Loon or two in the late fall and early winter. In the woods surrounding the lake you will find many species of woodpeckers, perhaps even Pileated Woodpeckers. Yellow-bellied Sapsuckers pass through in migration, but many spend the winter here. Carolina Chickadee, Tufted Titmouse, White-breasted Nuthatch, and Carolina Wren are permanent residents.

In the southwestern part of the city between Kauffman Road (Route FF) and Hutchinson Road just south of Brookline Road is the Southwest Sewage Treatment Plant on Wilson Creek; this attracts a variety of waterfowl from fall through winter and into the spring migration. A similar site on the north side of the city is the Fulbright Pumping Station. Drive north on M13 (Kansas Expressway) and exit at Stage Coach Road; then drive less than 1 mile east to reach the lake.

Two other lakes on the north side of the city are worth checking for waterfowl. McDaniel Lake can be reached by taking M13 north for about 3 miles. The lake is just east of the highway, north of Owens Road. To reach Fellows Lake, take U.S. 65 north for about 6 miles from the city limits, and then turn east on County Road A to reach the lake.

Several parks and cemeteries are worth visiting in May and September when migrants are passing through. Eastlawn Cemetery is just south of the Downtown Airport. Maple Park Cemetery is on Grand Street, 6 blocks west of the campus of Southwestern Missouri State University. At the intersection of Seminole Street and Glenstone Avenue (u.s. 60) the National Cemetery and the adjacent Hazelwood Cemetery also provide good havens for migrants after a night of passage. Also visit Phelps Grove Park, just south of Catalpa Street at Clay, during the same seasons.

If you have additional time, you can mix some birding with history and visit the Wilson's Creek Battlefield National Park. The major Civil War battle fought here in 1861 was an important encounter in the course of the war west of the Mississippi River. Although perhaps too manicured for many birders, the open second-growth parkland supports breeding White-eyed Vireos, Prairie Warblers, Yellow-breasted Chats, Indigo Buntings, Blue Grosbeaks, and Orchard Orioles. Take u.s. 60 (Sunshine Street) west from Springfield for about 5 miles and then turn south on County Road zz to reach the national park.

STOCKTON, MISSOURI

While the terrestrial habitats near this town in Cedar County are not especially noteworthy, Lake Stockton and the Stockton Sewage Ponds do provide good opportunities for waterbirds during spring and fall migration as well as in the winter.

To reach the sewage ponds, go east on M32 from the center of town to the intersection with Highway J and turn left. Continue for 0.2 mile and turn left again on Owen Mill Road and proceed for 0.4 mile, and turn left on Lee Hopkins Drive. Go 0.2 mile and stop on the hill to look over the three ponds for grebes and ducks.

Lake Stockton is surrounded by uplands of oak-hickory forest interspersed with meadows and cultivated lands. To reach the lake, proceed south on M39 from its junction with Highway 32 in Stockton for 0.8 mile and then turn left on Route RB and continue for 0.5 mile. At this point turn right at the sign indicating the entrance to the Stockton and Orleans Trail Recreation Areas and then off this main road follow the various roads that provide access to the lower end of the reservoir. To reach Stockton State Park and the upper reaches of the lake, return to M39, turn left and continue for 2.8 miles to the junction with M215. Turn left here and continue across the bridge over the lake for 6 miles to the office of the state park. A number of side roads will allow you to explore the terrestrial habitats and the lake shore within the park area.

FOREST-PRAIRIE MOSAIC

APPLETON CITY, MISSOURI

One of the best sites from among the many parcels of tall-grass prairie preserved throughout the forest-prairie mosaic in Missouri is the four-square-mile Taberville Prairie. This location is visited not only by bird watchers but also by botanists, lepidopterists, and a variety of natural history buffs. Although the typical breeding species of the prairie are usually gone by late September, the best times to come are from late March through November in order to catch the periods of spring and fall migration. Raptor passage can be especially exciting, since they often come over in large numbers, and during these times more northern grassland species, like Sprague's Pipits, Baird's Sparrows, and Le Conte's Sparrows, have been found here.

To reach this area, take M52 east from Butler MO or west from Clinton MO to reach Appleton City. Then go 1.5 miles east of town on M52 and turn right (south) on Route A. This county road turns east in 2 miles, but continue south on Route H. In about 6 miles this road intersects Route B, but continue for 1 mile south to the entrance to Taberville Prairie on your left. This gravel road into the prairie is a little less than 1 mile in length. In past years, from mid-March until the end of April, the Missouri Department of Conservation has placed a blind near the end of this road, from which you can watch the display of the Greater Prairie-chicken on a booming ground that has been used for over a hundred years (check with departmental personnel for availability). It is important that you enter the blind at least one hour before sunrise so that you are in the blind before the chickens arrive about half an hour later.

You can tell the activity on the lek begins to wane when the males start acting as if they were feeding and even sitting down for a few moments instead of fending off encroachment into their small territories by adjacent males. You can then feel free to leave the blind, even though you will flush the birds. Then follow some of the trails across the prairie. Henslow's Sparrows and Dickcissels will be here by late April, and Grasshopper Sparrows and Upland Sandpipers will arrive even earlier. Short-eared Owls winter here and may remain into late spring before migrating a little farther north to breed. Expect Northern Harriers at all seasons; they remain to nest when rodent populations are high.

Drive away from the prairie on the road by which you entered. In the breeding season you should hear Bell's Vireos singing in the hedgerows along the fence, while Scissor-tailed Flycatchers may be perched on the wires. Lark Sparrows also occur in the breeding season, while Harris' and White-crowned Sparrows will be along the fence in the fall and winter. When you get back to Route H, turn right (north) toward Appleton City. After 1 mile north, turn right (east) on Route B and then south on the first gravel road to your right. This road, paralleling the eastern border of Taberville Prairie, is a good birding road in the breeding season with Blue Grosbeaks and Indigo Buntings, Orchard and Northern Orioles, and Gray Catbirds and Northern Mockingbirds in second-growth timber. Also be alert for Prairie Warblers, Yellow-breasted Chats, and Yellow Warblers. In grassy patches along the road, stop and listen for Sedge Wrens. At 3 miles from Route B, this road makes a "T" with Route BB. Turn right (west) and go 1.5 miles to return to Route H.

With a snap of his head the Henslow's Sparrow sings his two-bits worth, announcing his territorial rights to a patch of unburned tall-grass prairie.

BUFFALO, KANSAS

This town is about 14 miles south of Yates Center on U.S. 75. Wilson County State Fishing Lake is just off U.S. 75 about 1.5 miles farther south. Although some waterfowl can be found on the lake at virtually all times of the year, the scrubby, second-growth areas that surround the lake make a visit here more productive during spring, summer, and fall. The gravel road that enters the area north off U.S. 75 circles the lake over a distance of about 3 miles and affords good views of the lake surface. In the fall the stands of sumac, dogwood, and osage orange provide excellent habitat for sparrows, and Harris', White-crowned, Tree, Song, Lincoln, and Swamp Sparrows occur in abundance. Many of these species linger into winter. In summer months watch for both Indigo and Painted Buntings, and Blue Grosbeaks are fairly common. In the dogwood patches, expect nesting Field Sparrows and Bell's Vireos.

40

Forest-Prairie
Mosaic

Just north of this town along the Neosho River is the John Redmond Reservoir, a lake developed by the U.S. Army Corps of Engineers which attracts a variety of waterfowl during the migratory seasons as well as during the winter until freeze. To reach the area around the dam, proceed north on U.S. 75 from the traffic light in Burlington. At 4.7 miles from the traffic light, turn left at New Strawn; go another 1.3 miles, and then turn right into the Damsite Public Use Area. This is a developed campground; thus, the terrestrial habitats are not especially attractive to birds, but the area provides good access for waterfowl viewing near the dam.

The best birding around John Redmond Reservoir is on the 18,500 acres of the Flint Hills National Wildlife Refuge at the upstream end of the lake. Almost 300 species of birds have been recorded there, of which 88 have been documented as nesting. All the expected waterfowl can be found during migration, and even Tundra Swans occasionally turn up. The shorebird list is good, and numbers of the more common species like Long-billed Dowitcher, Baird's Sandpiper, and other "peeps" can be impressive. The lake appears attractive to vagrant gulls; Little Gull, Glaucous Gull, and Black-legged Kittiwake have all been observed. Nesting passerines of note include Tree Swallow, Bell's Vireo, Prothonotary Warbler, and Painted Bunting.

To reach the wildlife refuge, continue north on U.S. 75 for 3.2 miles beyond the road to New Strawn. Then turn left (west) onto a gravel road. You will come to a stop sign at 2.2 miles; turn right to continue on the main east-west road along the north side of the lake which traverses upland tall-grass prairie in excellent condition. Look for Upland Sandpipers on the fenceposts as well as Eastern Meadowlarks, Grasshopper Sparrows, and Dickcissels, with Eastern Kingbirds and Scissor-tailed Flycatchers near trees, and Bell's Vireos in brushy thickets along the road. At 4.2 miles from your turn-off from U.S. 75 you will cross the road to Ottumwa. Two miles beyond this crossroad, turn left and continue 1.2 miles to the parking area for the Dove Roost Pond Trail that circles a small pond set in an upland area of elm, honey locust, cedar, black walnut, and hackberry. A branch off this trail

"Tweedle-deedle-dee, tweedle-deedle-dum . . ." under the cover of a plum
thicket, the feisty Bell's Vireo is more easily heard than seen. But a few
"swishes" will bring him out to investigate your intrusion.

to the right takes you to the Eagle Roost overlook, where from
November to March you should scan this arm of John Redmond
Lake for wintering eagles. It would also be worthwhile to walk
the roads and jeep trails in the immediate vicinity of the parking
area to explore the upland habitats at this site.

From the parking area, return to the main east-west road, turn
left (west) and continue for 0.9 mile at which point the road
bends to the right; you should turn left, followed by another immediate left, and proceed south for 1 mile. This stretch of the
road may be difficult to travel in wet weather, and it becomes
impossible, even in dry weather, beyond the sign on your right,
"road not maintained beyond this point." Do not drive any farther because the margins of this road are soft, and depending on
the lake level good birding begins just a few feet down the road.
So walk the road south as far as you can into the Goose Bend
Marsh area, stopping from time to time to scan the shallow water
and extensive mud flats on both sides of the road for shorebirds,
waterfowl, and herons, depending upon the season.

Return to the main gravel road. At this point you can leave the
area by continuing straight ahead through the town of Lebo to I-
35 about 8.5 miles to the north. Otherwise turn left. In about 0.5
mile you will cross a creek with riparian forest along its margins

that can be investigated. Because Pileated Woodpeckers are near the northwestern limit of their range in Kansas in the riparian forest of the Flint Hills National Wildlife Refuge, this and all other good riparian forest stands should be checked for that woodpecker and other forest species.

Continue west for another 0.5 mile and turn left (south) on an all-weather gravel road. In 0.3 mile there is a parking lot on your left adjacent to a pond. Park here. Explore the area around the pond, then walk south on the road until you come to a "T" in the road. Take the left trail and follow it into an extensive area that is a patchwork of old fields, brushy thickets, and small stands of deciduous forest trees intermingled with cultivated fields. This is an excellent area for a variety of edge and wet meadow birds, like Sedge Wren and Common Yellowthroat. Prothonotary Warblers nest in the swampy woods below the pond.

Return north from the parking lot to the point where you turned off the east-west road; continue north for another 0.5 mile and turn left to proceed west again. In 1 mile you will come to a creek. To your left is an extensive stand of riparian deciduous forest. Park beyond the bridge and walk along the west side of the creek where the trees are larger. This is another spot where the Pileated Woodpecker and other forest birds can be expected, and the edges are especially good for migrant passerines. Return to your car and continue west, stopping from time to time to investigate appropriate habitats along the road. In 3 miles you will cross the Neosho River and enter the town of Hartford. You can obtain a bird checklist and maps at refuge headquarters, 3 blocks west of Hartford High School. From Hartford you can reach I-35 via K130 through Neosho Rapids.

Forest-Prairie
Mosaic

CLINTON, MISSOURI

Montrose Lake Wildlife Management Area has been developed around the upper end of a cooling water lake for a generating facility of the Kansas City Power and Light Company. There are no extensive stands of upland deciduous forest on the site because the terrestrial habitats are largely forest edge and fence-rows with a narrow margin of riparian forest along the lakeshore to which access is limited. But Montrose Lake is worth visiting during the migratory periods and in the winter, given the variety of waterfowl that can be seen here.

To reach the lake, proceed west on M18 for 12.8 miles beyond its junction with Business 13 in Clinton and turn left (south) on Route RA. This road passes through private lands characteristic of the prairie-forest mosaic, and you should watch the roadsides not only for typical species but also for surprises like the Scissor-tailed Flycatcher, which arrives early enough and stays late enough to be coincident with part of the waterfowl migration. The road then crosses a railroad and comes to the headquarters of the wildlife area 3.5 miles from Route 18. At 0.5 mile beyond the headquarters area the road crosses a causeway over the upper end of the lake. To your right (west) are marshy areas along the lake margins, and to your left (east) is the open water of the lake. A better view of the lake can be obtained by driving another 0.5 mile beyond the bridge; turn left on a road that reaches the southern shore of the lake in 0.7 mile.

You can return to Clinton the way you came or turn left as you drive back from the south shore and continue for 3.6 miles to the junction with M52 in the town of Montrose. At this point you can continue to other birding sites at Taberville Prairie (Appleton City MO) and the Schell-Osage Wildlife Management Area (Nevada MO).

Another excellent tour is to Truman Reservoir, southeast of Clinton. Completed in 1979, the Truman Dam has created a 5 million acre-feet lake on the Osage and Grand rivers that lies in the transition zone between the oak-hickory forests to the north, the forest-prairie mosaic to the west, and the Ozark forest to the south. Birds characteristic of all three communities can be dis-

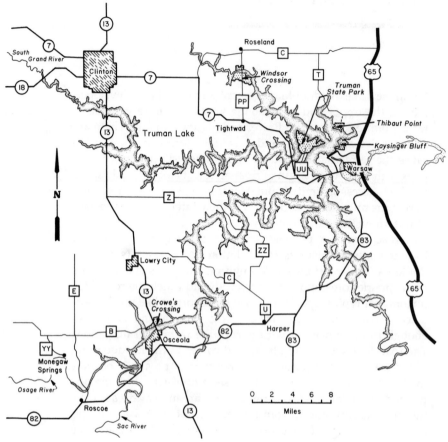

MAP 5. *Truman Lake*

covered here any time of the year, but April through October is the most productive period.

To begin a circular route that will take you to some of the best birding sites around the lake, go south from Clinton on M13 towards Lowry City. Just south of Clinton you cross the South Grand River and then, in another two miles or so, Deepwater Creek. The bridges over these branches of the lake afford the opportunity to check for waterfowl, and you also have a reasonably good chance of seeing a Pileated Woodpecker flying across the water into the heavy timber bordering the lake. In the breeding season, watch for Cliff Swallows nesting under the bridges. With a little exploring off the road and careful listening you can expect to find Yellow-throated and Warbling Vireos here as well as Northern Parulas. Yellow-throated and Cerulean Warblers, Eastern Phoebes, Great Crested and Acadian Flycatchers, and Eastern Wood-pewees are also possible.

Continue south through Lowry City to reach Crowe's Crossing and park your car so that you can walk through the woods here and listen for both Scarlet and Summer Tanagers as well as Wood Thrush during the breeding season. At any time of year you may see Black-capped or Carolina Chickadee, Tufted Titmouse, White-breasted Nuthatch, and Bewick's Wren; the Carolina Chickadee and Bewick's Wren are more common in parts of the forest with a greater Ozarkian aspect. If you walk down to the water in the spring and summer, you can expect House and Carolina Wrens, Bell's Vireo, Prothonotary and Kentucky Warblers, Louisiana Waterthrush, Common Yellowthroat, and American Redstart. Belted Kingfishers will usually "rattle" within a few minutes of your arrival at the water's edge, but be sure to keep an eye skyward for the Turkey Vulture and Red-shouldered, Broad-winged, and Red-tailed Hawks that are often overhead in this area.

From Crowe's Crossing, go west on County Road B, past the intersection with County Road E, to the junction with County Road YY. Turn left (south) here and drive to Monegaw Springs, on an unflooded section of the Osage River. In town, watch for Ruby-throated Hummingbirds and several different species of swallows. Then drive down toward the river, stopping at second-growth areas to listen for Prairie Warblers and White-eyed and Bell's Vireos. When you stand along the river you may see Mallards and Wood Ducks, and in summer you cannot miss the Northern Parulas and Prothonotary Warblers.

Return on Route YY to Route B, turn right (east) and drive 2.7 miles to Route E. Turn right (south) on E and continue across the Osage River to Roscoe and the junction with M82. Turn left here and go east past the intersection with M13 at Osceola to the junction with M83, 23 miles from Roscoe. This scenic highway takes you through a typical mix of prairie and oak-hickory forest with crossings over the Sac River and Weaubleau Creek arms of Truman Reservoir. Stop at inviting sites, but especially make the effort during the nesting season to check the brushier prairies for Blue Grosbeaks and Lark Sparrows. At M83, turn left to reach U.S. 65 at Warsaw. Turn left at this intersection and go north to the visitors' center at Kaysinger Bluff. This stop provides an excellent view of the entire eastern portion of the reservoir. In winter you may see Bald Eagles as well as a variety of waterbirds, including Pied-billed and Horned Grebes, Common Goldeneye, Bufflehead and Common and Hooded Mergansers. There is also a resident flock of Canada Geese on the lake.

From the visitors' center, return to U.S. 65 and continue north to reach County Road T. Turn left (west) on T and continue for a short distance to the road into Thibaut Point. This site also provides an excellent vantage for searching the lake for waterfowl in winter as well as during migration. Then return to Route T and continue to its junction with County Route C. In this landscape, a mix of prairie and agriculture lands, you should watch for Upland Sandpipers on the fence posts and Scissor-tailed Flycatchers and Loggerhead Shrikes on the utility wires. Seven miles from the junction of Routes T and C, turn left on County Route PP and continue south for 2 miles to Windsor Crossing. This public access area affords you the opportunity to search for waterfowl in the arm of the lake fed by Tebo Creek. Then continue south on PP for 4 miles to the town of Tightwad. At this point you can turn right (west) on M7 to return to Clinton.

If you would like to spend some time exploring oak-hickory upland to see such typical forest species as Northern Flicker, Red-headed, Red-bellied, Downy, and Hairy Woodpeckers, Blue Jay, Black-capped Chickadee, Tufted Titmouse, White-breasted Nuthatch, Blue-gray Gnatcatcher, tanagers, and Rufous-sided Towhee, turn left on M7 and drive 8 miles to the junction with County Route UU; turn left here and drive 3.5 miles to the Harry S Truman State Park. On spring and summer evenings, you will hear Whip-poor-wills in the forest. Chipping and Field Sparrows and other edge species can also be found here in appropriate habitats during the summer. You can return on M7 to Clinton, or you can take County Route z westward to M13 between Lowry City and Clinton.

47

Clinton,
Missouri

48

*Forest-Prairie
Mosaic*

The Kansas Department of Wildlife and Parks has developed an extensive area for public hunting along the Fall River and its tributaries, including a wide variety of habitats attractive to the bird watcher during all seasons. As with all similar areas, the birder should be considerate and not interfere with the pursuit of hunters, especially during waterfowl season.

To reach the Fall River Wildlife Management Area, take K99 south from its intersection with U.S. 54, 2 miles east of Eureka. Proceed for 6.5 miles and then turn left (east). At 1.6 miles from the turn-off the road crosses a bridge over Homer Creek. Just beyond the bridge turn on the road to the left, drive about 0.1 mile, and park on the left side in the old road bed. Take time to explore this riparian forest of hickory, oak, walnut, elm, and hackberry both upstream beyond the bridge and downstream.

Facing into the wind, the Scissor-tailed Flycatcher sits and waits, then sallies out. Using its long outer rectrices and slotting the wing, it turns, rises, and seizes its prey.

During migration the variety of passerines is excellent, and you should expect the characteristic species of the eastern deciduous forest in the summer and winter.

Return to the main road and turn left to continue east, skirting the riparian vegetation along the north side of Otter Creek, stopping to listen and look wherever it seems appropriate and parking for more extensive searches at the several turn-outs available along the road between the Fall River on your left and Otter Creek on your right. At 2.2 miles from the last corner the road crosses Otter Creek and continues south through a mix of wet prairie, cultivated fields, and old fields. At 0.8 mile beyond this bridge you come to a "T"; turn left and continue to the dead end at the Climax boatramp in 0.8 mile, stopping as you wish to search for birds in the excellent oldfield and prairie habitat along the road.

To return to K99, go straight west for 4.5 miles. If you would like to spend more time in the riparian forest along Otter Creek, turn right (north) and go just 0.1 mile to a primitive road to your left. If it is too wet to enter, park along the highway and walk in, but you can drive in during dry weather. The birds you will find here are similar to those you found along Homer Creek.

To reach Fall River Lake, turn left (south) at this intersection and go for 5.8 miles to its junction with K96. Turn left (east) on K96 and proceed for 7.5 miles; turn left and continue for 1 mile until a road branches off to the right. But continue straight ahead for 0.7 mile, entering the South Shore Area of Fall River State Park, to a crossroad. The characteristic bird of this developed area is the Scissor-tailed Flycatcher, which seem to be almost everywhere from spring through early fall. If you turn left here, follow the road to the North Rock Ridge Cove area (no permit required). The campground is reached in 2.5 miles and suffers from development, but the adjacent old fields and young deciduous forest habitat provide considerable edge and a variety of birds. If you turn right and follow Lakeshore Road, you will be afforded many good vantage points for waterfowl viewing. In 1.5 miles you will come to a "T"; turn left here and then bear left at the next junction to follow the road over the spillway and dam to the eastern side of the lake. In the Quarry Bay area of the Fall River State Park there are patches of upland deciduous oak forest characteristic of the cross-timbers region.

Located west of this historic town near the Missouri border, Bourbon County State Fishing Lake is worth visiting in either May or September because the wood warbler migration can provide an interesting chance to find Black-and-white, Golden-winged, Magnolia, Black-throated Green, Chestnut-sided, Bay-breasted, Wilson's, Blackpoll, and Canada Warblers, as well as both waterthrushes and Ovenbird in the upland hardwoods and brushy second-growth stands associated with this small lake. June is productive, too; during the summer both Yellow Warbler and Common Yellowthroat can be found in the willows along the margins of the lake, while Northern Parula and Kentucky Warbler nest in the heavier forest sites. In second-growth along the lake in the breeding season you will find Bell's Vireo, Yellow-breasted Chat, and Indigo Bunting.

To reach the lake from Fort Scott, drive west on u.s. 54 for 19 miles to the town of Bronson. At the intersection with northbound k3, turn left and go south for about 7 miles. The lake is small, and you can drive all the way around it, a distance of about 5 miles. In the agricultural lands adjacent to the park you will find Horned Lark, Dickcissel, Field Sparrow, Grasshopper Sparrow, and possibly Lark Sparrow during the breeding season. Also, both Eastern and Western Meadowlarks are resident in this area. Although the area is not especially good for waterfowl, check for herons and waders if low water exposes mud flat habitat.

INDEPENDENCE, KANSAS

The Verdigris River flows southward into Oklahoma along the eastern border of the Chautauqua Hills. One of its major tributaries, the Elk River, has been dammed just west of this city in Montgomery County to form Elk City Lake, a U.S. Army Corps of Engineers impoundment, where spring and fall waterfowl migrations can be spectacular. Furthermore, as evidenced from the longstanding annual Christmas Bird Counts, waterfowl concentrations remain high all winter, except in the most severe years. Lying in the cross-timbers area, the uplands of oak and hickory surrounding the lake provide excellent habitat for woodpeckers, flycatchers, jays, and tanagers in breeding season; but in winter, mixed species flocks of both Ruby-crowned and Golden-crowned Kinglets, Brown Creeper, Tufted Titmouse, Carolina Chickadee, and White-breasted Nuthatch move through the forests. And the spring and fall wood warbler migrations are almost as rich as they are farther east in the Ozark Forest. Although a visit in almost any month will reward you with a species list characteristic of the season, April, May, June, September, and October are probably the best times for viewing.

To begin your tour, drive west from Independence on u.s. 75 / u.s. 160. Continue west on u.s. 160 for 4 miles beyond the point where u.s. 75 turns south, and then turn right (north) at a well-marked intersection on a hardtop road to reach the Card Creek Recreation Area. During the fall and winter, the road into Card Creek should be checked for flocks of sparrows. At 1.3 miles from u.s. 160 the road turns left (west) for a short distance and then bends north again, reaching the Card Creek area 3 miles from the highway. In all seasons be sure to check the narrow inlets, and especially the area with the standing dead trees, for Wood Ducks; and in the spring and summer, listen and look for nesting Prothonotary Warblers.

Return to u.s. 160 and continue west. The highway crosses Coon Creek and tributaries of Card Creek, but the best place to stop and explore the floodplain forest in the wildlife management area is where the highway crosses the Elk River, approximately 5 miles from the road into Card Creek. In this high-quality habitat you should expect to see Pileated Woodpeckers

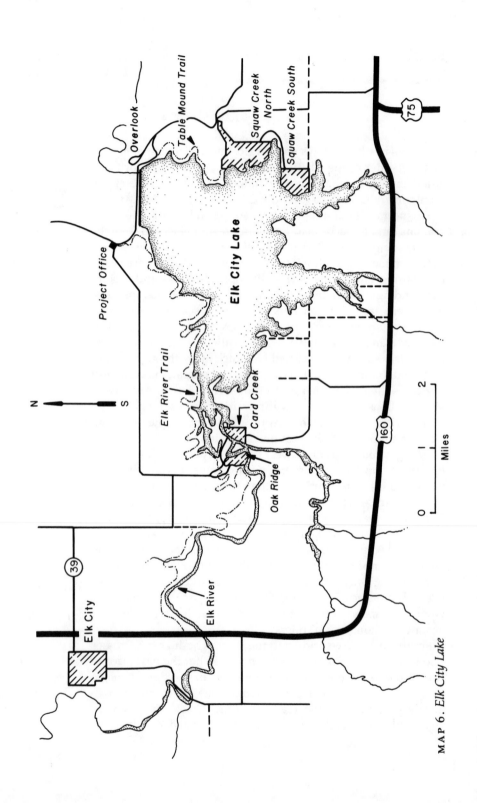

MAP 6. *Elk City Lake*

and Red-shouldered Hawks at any season; during migration keep alert for Broad-winged Hawks. Less than a half mile north of the river you can walk along a section of the hiking trail, beginning on the east side of the highway and providing access to this part of the wildlife area. Then return to your car and continue north on u.s. 160 for 2 miles, turn right on k39, and continue east for 1.5 miles. At this corner, k39 turns north, but you should turn right (south), staying on the hardtop for 2.5 miles, where you come to a "T" in the road. Turn right here and proceed for about 1 mile to reach the Oak Ridge Recreation Area. The oaks and hickories at this site are quite tall and provide excellent habitat for Red-headed, Red-bellied, Hairy, and Downy Woodpeckers. In the breeding season these species are joined by both Scarlet and Summer Tanagers, Great Crested Flycatchers, Eastern Wood-pewees, Blue-gray Gnatcatchers, and Kentucky Warblers. Just before entering this area, a crossing of the Elk River Hiking Trail parallels the channel of the Elk River east for 4.5 miles, ending at the Project Office. The trail, snaking through uplands of oak and hickory, provides the hiker with both excellent views of the main body of the lake and good exposure to typical cross-timbers habitat.

When you leave the Oak Ridge area, watch for Eastern Bluebird in the more open sections of the woodlands along the road and continue straight north through the "T." The road turns east, and in about 4 miles from this intersection you reach the Corps of Engineers Project Office where you can obtain an area map. Now follow the road across the dam and turn left to reach the overlook. From this vantage point you can view the lake and expect a variety of puddle duck species as well as Canvasback, Redhead, Ring-necked Duck, Lesser Scaup, Bufflehead, and Common Goldeneye; in spring and fall there will also be flocks of American White Pelicans. It is also worthwhile to take the Post Oak Nature Trail, a short 30- to 45-minute loop, from the parking lot. The Table Mound Hiking Trail also departs from the overlook and follows the east shore of the lake to the camping area in the Squaw Creek North area of the State Park. When you leave the overlook, continue south on the main road. At the entrance to the state park, you can either enter the park (permit required) by turning right or bear right at the fork to continue south on the hardtop, reaching u.s. 160 in about 2.7 miles. If you choose to enter the state park, follow the signs to Squaw Creek South for a good view of this arm of the lake.

When you reach U.S. 160, turn left (east) to return to Independence. In the center of town turn right on Montgomery County 3900 (Tenth Street) and drive south for almost 4 miles, turning left on a hard surfaced road to reach the Montgomery County State Fishing Lake. Although the lake is fairly small, it does attract some waterfowl. In spring and summer the vegetation around the lake is a good place to look for Bell's and White-eyed Vireos, Painted and Indigo Buntings, as well as Blue Grosbeak. In fall and winter you will find large numbers of Harris' and White-crowned Sparrows.

Forest-Prairie
Mosaic

KANSAS CITY, KANSAS

Just about one mile south of the Missouri River in the north-western section of Kansas City KS, a large, deep-water lake in Wyandotte County Park attracts large numbers of migrant waterfowl, including both puddle and diving ducks. In the fall Ospreys join the Bald Eagles that remain into winter. In the oak-hickory woods surrounding the lake you will find a limited, but characteristic bird community of woodpeckers, tits, jays, and nuthatches. The diversity of migrant warblers, however, is often high. To reach this park from downtown Kansas City, go west on Leavenworth Road (K5) for 9 miles from the I-635 exit and turn right on K5 as it enters the park. You can also exit I-435 on Leavenworth Road and go about 1 mile east, turning left on K5 into the park.

Shawnee Mission Park lake also attracts waterfowl, and the park provides forested uplands for migrant passerines. During the breeding season, the open woods provide edge habitat for nesting species, such as Field Sparrow and Indigo Bunting. To reach this site, return to Leavenworth Road, turn right (west) to I-435, and enter the southbound lanes of I-435. Continue south across the Kansas River and exit I-435 west on 87th Street. The park entrance is on your right, about 1.5 miles west of the interchange.

An alternate route to Shawnee Mission Park is by way of the bottomlands along the Kansas River near Bonner Springs. In fall and spring you may see Bonaparte's, Ring-billed, and Herring Gulls along the river with Black Terns present in mid- and late May. Less frequently seen species like Thayer's and Glaucous Gulls have turned up along this stretch of the river in winter; Bald Eagles can be expected on most visits at this time of year. Going south on I-435 from Leavenworth Road, exit after 2 miles on U.S. 24 (State Street) toward the west and continue for about 5 miles to K7. Turn left on K7, go south through Bonner Springs, and exit the highway to stop along the river to check for waterbirds. Then continue south on K7, being sure to scan flooded fields in spring and fall for waders. It would also be worthwhile to stop and carefully check alfalfa fields along the highway in March and April for Lesser Golden Plovers and for Buff-breasted

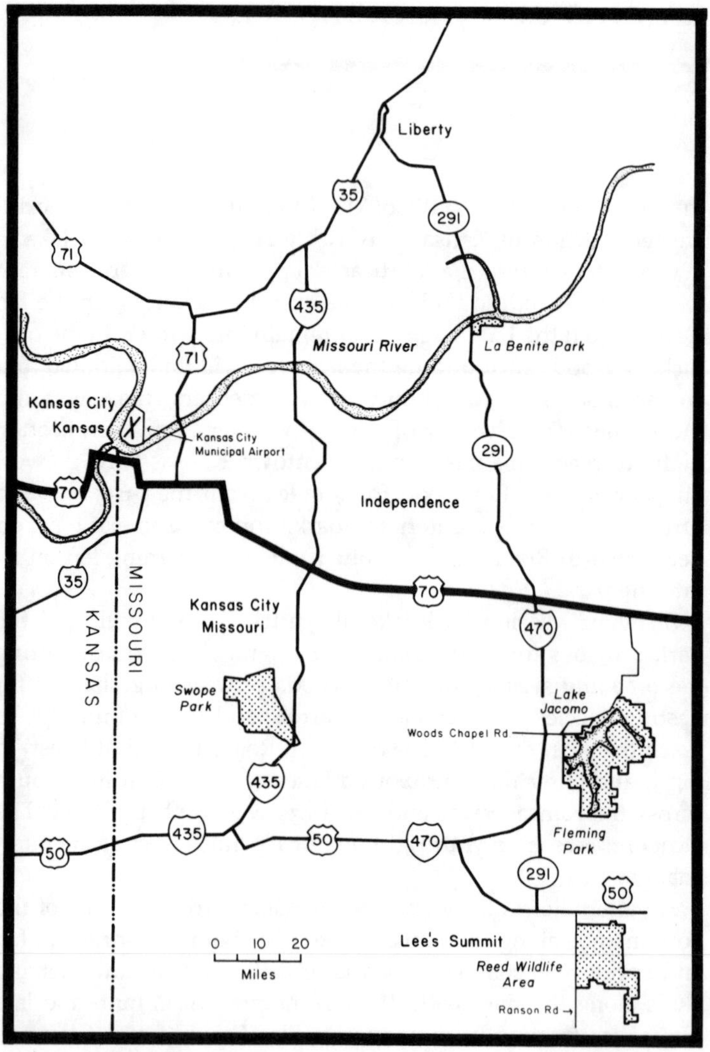

MAP 7. *Kansas City Metropolitan Area*

Sandpipers from mid-August to early September. During late summer and early fall, these fields often attract Bobolinks. To reach the park, exit K7 on 83rd Street (Craig Road) about 8.5 miles south of the river. Go east (the road eventually becomes 87th Street) and enter the park about 3 miles from the K7 turn-off.

57

Kansas City, Kansas

Metropolitan Kansas City, with over a million inhabitants, still offers a variety of interesting places to visit for bird watching. Spring and fall seasons can be thoroughly delightful; temperatures are moderate, and precipitation generally presents no major problems. If your visit to Kansas City is a planned layover at Kansas City International Airport with just enough time to visit nearby sites, try the Missouri River oxbow lakes described under this heading as well as Weston Bend bottoms (Leavenworth KS) or Smithville Lake and Trimble Wildlife Area (Smithville MO).

Swope Park, located in the southeastern section of the city, contains within its more than 1,000 acres both oak-hickory forest and riparian forest along the Blue River that offer good habitat for both nesting and migrant passerines. In the summer you should find Whip-poor-will, Great Crested Flycatcher, Eastern Wood-pewee, Carolina Wren, Wood Thrush, Blue-gray Gnatcatcher, Yellow-throated and Red-eyed Vireos, and Summer Tanager. In the riparian habitats, check for Acadian Flycatcher, Warbling Vireo, Northern Parula, Louisiana Waterthrush, and Cerulean Warbler. Wood Ducks nest here as well. During May and September, warbler migration can be impressive with possibly more than twenty species; Tennessee and Nashville are the most common. Some of the less frequently observed species you can still expect to see include Black-throated Green, Blackburnian, Bay-breasted, and Mourning Warblers. Swope Park is easily reached by leaving I-435 at Gregory Boulevard and proceeding west. A stop at the Nature Center, just a little over a mile from this exit, to talk with the helpful park personnel will aid you in finding the best spots in the park to bird. Gregory takes you past one of the two lakes in the park where waterfowl often rest. The other lake can be reached by turning right on Lewis Road. This route will also bring you close to the riparian habitats along the Blue River.

Another surprisingly good place to visit is Downtown Airport in the bottoms on the opposite bank from the confluence of the Kansas River with the Missouri River. Grassy areas between the runways and taxiways of the airfield attract Upland Sandpipers in spring and fall, and in fall and winter you may see Short-eared

Owls and Northern Harriers. Rough-legged Hawks join these and other raptors in winter if rodent populations are high. Winter also affords the chance to see mixed flocks of Horned Larks and longspurs, almost within the shadow of downtown skyscrapers. While you are not allowed onto the field, Richards Road and Lou Holland Drive encircle the airport and provide vantage points. In the summer you will see both Eastern and Western Kingbirds sitting on the boundary fence or on the navigational towers, one of the few places in Missouri where Western Kingbirds regularly nest. To reach the airport, take Broadway from downtown north across the Missouri River (toll bridge) to reach Richards Road. Continue past the terminal areas and turn left onto Lou Holland Drive to circle the airfield.

A number of lakes cut off by the meandering Missouri in the bottomlands along the Missouri side of the river can be reached from Kansas City; they are well worth visiting at any time of year. Although the periods of waterfowl and shorebird migration perhaps will provide a more spectacular experience, the breeding season is excellent because the marsh habitat present in these shallow oxbow lakes is uncommon in the area. If recent rainfall has been sufficient, you should check the numerous ponds in the flooded fields along the way for migrant waterbirds.

To reach the three most-birded lakes, take U.S. 71/I-35 north from downtown Kansas City, crossing the Missouri River on the Paseo Bridge. Continue on U.S. 71 as it turns west now with I-29 towards St. Joseph. Just beyond the junction with I-635, exit the highway on NW 64th Street (M45) and go west. About 11 miles beyond the city limits, just south of Farley MO on M45, you will reach the first of these oxbows, Horseshoe Lake. Then continue beyond Farley to Beverly MO where the terrain between the highway and the river is particularly susceptible to flooding; hence, it is a great habitat for ducks and waders in the fall and spring. Continue north on M45 past the town of Weston for 13 miles beyond Beverly and just north of Bean Lake MO to reach Bean Lake. Bean Lake and the Little Bean Marsh Natural History Area, managed by the Missouri Department of Conservation, are the best natural marshes along the Missouri River, and the slough and riparian forest in the old river channel are well worth exploring for birds. Sugar Lake, just another 3 miles on M45, is adjacent to Lewis and Clark State Park (see Atchison KS).

The birds you will see at these oxbow lakes include all the puddle ducks, gulls and terns, waders, herons, egrets, and other species associated with cattail marsh habitat. During the summer, watch for breeding American and Least Bitterns as well as Great Egrets, Snowy Egrets, Little Blue Herons, both night herons, and the more common Great Blue and Green-backed Herons, all of which use these marshes as feeding areas. American Coots and an occasional Common Moorhen can be seen, along with both King and Black Rails which probably nest in these marshes. Be alert for Marsh Wrens in the cattails. In late fall expect flocks of American White Pelicans along with Snow, Canada, and Greater White-fronted Geese. Also in the fall, especially during September and October, you should see all the species of eastern swallows, with concentrations of Purple Martins and Tree Swallows sometimes reaching very large numbers. If you come in May, you will find both species of yellowlegs, Solitary and Spotted Sandpipers, and a variety of "peeps," especially Least, Semipalmated, Western, and Baird's Sandpipers, joined by a few Hudsonian Godwits and Wilson's Phalaropes. Toward the end of May and early June, the White-rumped Sandpipers replace the earlier peeps.

LAWRENCE, KANSAS

On the south side of Lawrence a wet meadow, approximately one-half square mile in area, known as Baker Wetlands lies north of the Wakarusa River between Louisiana and Haskell streets. The habitat is dominated by sedges and prairie cordgrass (*Spartina*) with patches of forbs and scattered islands of cottonwoods and willow. In the spring there is usually standing water, but through the summer the area becomes progressively drier. Bird finding here is satisfactory at all seasons, but can be exceptional when the habitat is suitable for attracting rails and shorebirds during migration. Northern Harriers have nested here, Sedge Wrens appear in late summer, and Marsh Wrens, LeConte's Sparrows, and Swamp Sparrows can be expected during fall migration in October. If some water is present and the weather has been mild, there is always the chance of discovering some wetland stragglers during the winter. Short-eared Owls are also a winter possibility.

To reach this site, take u.s. 59 south out of Lawrence for 1.5 miles south of the intersection of u.s. 59 and k10. Turn left (east) on 31st Street and continue for another 1.5 miles. Then turn right on the Baker Wetlands entrance road that dead-ends almost immediately at a locked gate. Park here, climb the gate, and cross a drainage canal that borders the site on the north. This canal is diked on the south side, and you should walk this dike during the migration seasons, since the elms, hackberries, and honey locusts provide excellent cover for passerines. The dike also provides a vantage point to overlook the wetter areas. The entrance road bisects the area north and south; walk it to explore the area more thoroughly. You will also then discover another road that bisects the area east and west, providing further access to this wetlands oasis in a developed area.

Just a few miles to the west of Lawrence is Clinton Lake, a U.S. Army Corps of Engineers impoundment on the Wakarusa River. Like the other reservoirs developed throughout western Missouri and Kansas, the open water attracts a variety of waterbirds during migration and in the ice-free periods of winter, including a substantial population of Bald Eagles from November to April. Additionally, public areas provide for waterfowl viewing and en-

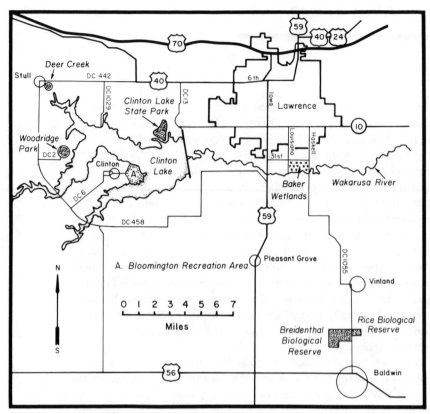

MAP 8. *Lawrence Area*

try into some delightful stands of upland oak-hickory forest and riparian forests along the stream drainages that enter the lake.

Start a rewarding bird tour around the lake by driving west from Lawrence on u.s. 40 (Sixth Street). Continue 4 miles beyond the junction of u.s. 40 and u.s. 59 (Iowa Street) and turn left (south) on Douglas Co. 13, reaching the entrance to Clinton Lake State Park (permit required) 1.8 miles on your right. From here you can survey the lower part of the lake just behind the dam.

To reach the upper end of the lake and a greater variety of habitats, return on Douglas Co. 13 to u.s. 40, turn left (west), continue for 2 miles to Douglas Co. 442, and bear left toward the town of Stull. You will see a sign indicating the Clinton Wildlife Management Area on your right at this intersection. Proceed west on Douglas Co. 442 for 1.6 miles and then turn left (south) on Douglas Co. 1029. After 2.3 miles you will reach a parking lot and boat ramp on Clinton Lake. At this point many standing dead trees in the water provide perching sites for Bald Eagles in winter and Ospreys during both spring and fall migrations. It would also be worthwhile to explore the fencerow and oldfield habitats along the lakeshore that you can reach on foot from this parking lot. This is especially good habitat for wintering Harris', White-crowned, White-throated, Lincoln's, and Song Sparrows.

Return to Douglas Co. 442, turn left, and continue west for another 2.5 miles where you will find another parking lot on your left. At this point you are above the conservation pool level of the lake, but if you park here you can walk down into part of the Clinton Wildlife Management Area composed of a patchwork of cultivated fields, fencerows, and old fields along the Deer Creek drainage. You can expect to find the birds of weed fields and edge typical for the season of your visit.

A little farther west on Douglas Co. 442 you will come to the junction with Douglas Co. 1023 in the town of Stull. Turn left (south) on 1023 and continue for 3.5 miles, turn left (east) on Douglas Co. 2 for 1 mile, and then turn left (north) for about 0.5 mile to reach Woodridge Park, a primitive campground maintained by the Corps of Engineers (no fee). Walk north from the parking area into an excellent stand of mature oak-hickory forest along the ridge and on the slope above Dry Creek. This is the best example of upland deciduous forest around the lake and should be visited whenever you come to Clinton Lake, whether for nesting species like Red-eyed Vireo, Summer Tanager, Kentucky Warbler, and Rose-breasted Grosbeak or a variety of thrushes, vireos, and warblers during migration or mixed-species flocks of chickadees, titmice, creepers, nuthatches, and kinglets in winter. The entrance road beyond the turn-off into the park is blocked, but you can walk as it continues north, eventually dropping down to Dry Creek bordered by a riparian forest of elm, buckeye, and sycamore. Like the uplands, this part of the site provides excellent birding during migration and in winter as well as such nesting species as Indigo Bunting, Blue Grosbeak, and Louisiana Waterthrush during the breeding season.

To continue your circuit of the lake, return to Douglas Co. 1023 and turn left (south). About 1.5 miles from this corner you will approach a bridge over an arm of the lake. Turn off at a parking lot to your right just before you get to the bridge; this is also part of the Clinton Wildlife Management Area. To the west of the bridge the shallow water is good for waders and puddle ducks at the appropriate seasons. East of the bridge deeper water attracts diving ducks.

Beyond this bridge and about 6.4 miles south of Stull on Douglas Co. 1023, turn left (northeast) on Douglas Co. 6 towards the town of Clinton. At 3.6 miles from this intersection you will reach the entrance to the Bloomington Recreation Area, a developed campground on a peninsula jutting out between the main arms of Clinton Lake and providing excellent access for waterfowl viewing.

Return on Douglas Co. 6 and turn left on 1023. You will soon cross another bridge over the southernmost arm of the lake. Douglas Co. 1023 turns off, but continue on Douglas Co. 458; 3.4 miles from the intersection with Douglas Co. 6 you can reach Rockhaven Park by turning left onto a gravel road and continuing to the parking lot in the campground 1.3 miles from the turn-off. The upland habitat here is much like that of Woodridge Park, but this site lacks the riparian aspect. Furthermore, it appears more heavily used, especially by horsepeople. The loop around Clinton Lake can be completed by driving east beyond the entrance road to Rockhaven Park on Douglas Co. 458 until intersecting U.S. 59 south of Lawrence in about 9 miles.

LEE'S SUMMIT, MISSOURI

Because of its proximity to a metropolitan area, the James A. Reed Memorial Wildlife Area is heavily used for fishing, hunting and other outdoor activities. Nevertheless, this 2,500-acre site is a good example of the mix of habitats in the forest-prairie mosaic, and its desirability for the bird watcher has been augmented by the development of eleven lakes, varying in size from 1 to 42 acres. Terrestrial habitats include patches of tall-grass prairie, cultivated crops planted to provide winter wildlife food, fencerows of oak, elm, and osage orange, old fields, and areas of upland oak-hickory forest. While some waterfowl are attracted to the lakes during migration, visitors to the Reed Wildlife Area at any time of year will see a representative sample of the birds that characterize these habitats.

To reach this area, go east on U.S. 50 from Lee's Summit. At 1.3 miles east of the interchange of U.S. 50 and M291 north, turn right (south) on Ranson Road and proceed 1.5 miles to the entrance of the wildlife area on your left. Soon after you enter the area, you can pick up a map of the area in the visitors' center at the parking lot on your left. For the best mix of habitats, continue east on the entrance road for 1.6 miles to Bodarc Lake and the Shawnee Trace Trail that begins at the east end of the parking lot. From here you can hike through the site's largest stand of deciduous forest, composed of mature oak-hickory uplands and riparian hackberry and sycamore. After entering the trail, you eventually reach a suspension bridge where a trail comes in on your right. If you continue across the bridge, you will make a loop through a variety of habitats, coming back to this junction. In winter search the conifers on the south side of Bodarc Lake for Long-eared and Northern Saw-whet Owls.

Expect a greater diversity of waterfowl during migration and in the winter at the 940-acre Lake Jacomo in Fleming Park. This lake is probably the most reliable site for migrant loons and grebes in the Kansas City area. Even Western Grebes have been seen here during late fall and early winter. Particularly in the fall, you will find diving ducks like Canvasback, Redhead, Ring-necked Duck, and Lesser Scaup. During the winter, you can expect Common Goldeneye, Bufflehead, Ruddy Duck, and Common and Hooded Mergansers. And there is always the chance for Oldsquaw, Greater Scaup, and scoters. Although most of the approximately 4,000 acres of the park is mowed grass, the hillsides around the lake support an oak-hickory forest, and there is some riparian forest in the creek valleys draining into the lake. During the breeding season you should expect to find Great Crested Flycatcher, Eastern Wood-pewee, Carolina Wren, Wood Thrush, Red-eyed Vireo, Northern Parula, Kentucky Warbler, and Indigo Bunting as well as the more common resident forest passerines.

In winter stands of planted conifers in the park support small populations of kinglets, Red-breasted Nuthatches, American Goldfinches, Pine Siskins, and occasionally White-winged and Red Crossbills. Furthermore, with a slow and careful check through the rows of trees you might come across a Great Horned Owl, Long-eared Owl, or Eastern Screech-owl.

To reach Lake Jacomo, exit U.S. 50 on M291 north. Continue as this highway joins I-470 about 3 miles north and then exit east 2.5 miles farther north on Woods Chapel Road. In 1.7 miles you come to the entrance to the park. Then follow any of the roads around the lake either to gain access for waterfowl viewing or to hike through the forested habitats. While you are at Fleming Park, be sure to stop at the Burroughs Audubon Society library, usually open for a few hours daily. The library is staffed by knowledgeable personnel who can answer your questions about local birds and identify other places in the area to see them.

NEVADA, MISSOURI

The riparian forest along the Osage River in the Schell-Osage Wildlife Management Area is one of the best examples of this habitat as well as one of the more accessible stands of floodplain vegetation in western Missouri; hence, it is worth a visit any time of the year. Pileated Woodpeckers are common permanent residents, and Prothonotary and Cerulean Warblers, Northern Parula, Red-eyed and Yellow-throated Vireos, Blue-gray Gnatcatcher, Scarlet Tanager, and Rose-breasted Grosbeak can be found during the breeding season. The impoundments on the site provide extensive marsh and open-water habitats that attract a wide variety of waterfowl and shorebirds in addition to herons and egrets, gulls and terns, rails, and marsh-nesting passerines. A visit to this site in late April or early May should produce a bird list of more than one hundred species.

Drive east on u.s. 54 for 12 miles from the intersection with u.s. 71 just north of Nevada and turn left (north) on Highway AA. Continue through the town of Dederick and after 11.4 miles turn right (east) on Route RA. At 1.5 miles from this corner, turn right to reach the headquarters where you can obtain a map of the area, but a bird checklist is not currently available. A good example of a riparian forest of oak, hickory, and sycamore can be reached by turning right (east) as you come back out from headquarters and continue for 2 miles, passing entrances to campground areas on both your left and right. Turn left and then right at the first opportunity on a road that passes between Barbour Lake on your left and the Osage River on your right. Continue on this road for about a mile, park, and take any side trail to your left that will lead you into the forest.

Another stand of riparian forest can be explored in the area below the dam of Atkinson Lake. Instead of turning left after you pass the entrances to the two campground areas off the road heading east from the headquarters, turn right, continue across the dam, and park where convenient. Beyond the point where a road branches off to the right, this road parallels the Osage River at a distance of about one-half mile and then dead-ends after 1 mile. You can gain access to the bottomlands from this road as well.

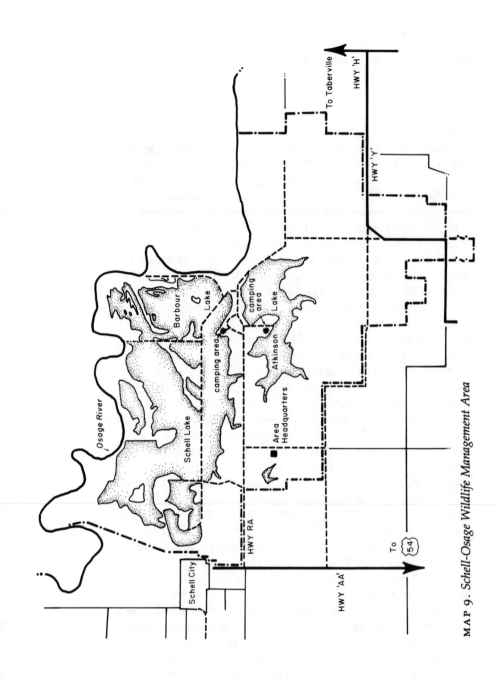

MAP 9. *Schell-Osage Wildlife Management Area*

The ringing "sweet, sweet, sweet, . . ." of the Prothonotary Warbler can
now be heard where farmers' cattle once grazed as nest sites are selected in
the ghost forest flooded by the impounded waters of the reservoir.

To survey the wetlands on the site, follow the road east from
the headquarters road and turn left beyond the campgrounds;
but instead of turning right at the first road, continue on as the
road passes between open water on the south and extensive
marsh and shallow pool areas on the north. Several roads on
your right permit you to turn off and park for a better look. When
water levels are low, the extensive mudflats attract a variety of
shorebirds. In about 2 miles a road to your left takes you back to
Route RA in 0.5 mile at a point approximately 0.5 mile west of
the headquarters road, thus permitting you to make a complete
loop. But before you take this road, continue all the way to the
end of the road you are on to complete your exploration of the
area.

70
_____

Forest-Prairie
Mosaic

The upper end of Perry Lake offers a variety of habitats that makes a birding trip to this site rewarding during any season. The lake provides open water for ducks and geese, the load of silt flowing down the Delaware River has built up extensive mud flats that attract large numbers of shorebirds and other waders, and the Kansas Department of Wildlife and Parks has developed a series of excellent marshes that not only make good duck habitat but also offer the ecological requirements for herons, rails, and probably the best concentration of breeding Sedge Wrens in the region.

To begin the tour go west on K92 from its junction with K16 in Oskaloosa for 6.8 miles, then turn right (north) on a hardtop road towards the Paradise Point Recreation Area. Continue for 2 miles and then turn left (west) to reach the Paradise Point Area boundary in about 1.5 miles. You can make a left turn here to go into the picnic area, which provides a good vantage point for viewing waterfowl on the open water south of the point. If you continue west for about another 1.5 miles, you will enter the campground area which also gives you access to the lakeshore on the south side of the point. If you take any of the several right turns off this main road, you will be able to scan the extensive mud flats deposited by the Delaware River as it flows into the lake. You will need a telescope, since you cannot walk out for a closer look because either water channels block your way or it is just too muddy.

Return east to the main north-south road and then turn left (north). At 2.7 miles north of the road from Paradise Point, the road borders a marsh area on your left, but it is best not to stop here; rather continue north for another 0.5 mile where there is a road into the Perry Wildlife Management Area on your left. Just pull off here and park; then walk the trail south through the flooded woodland of willow, elm, silver maple, and cottonwood to the marsh areas. Not only is this walk good for a variety of migrants during the spring and fall periods of passage, but Prothonotary Warblers, Northern Parulas, and Wood Ducks can be found as nesting species during the summer. Return to your car and continue for another mile north where a gravel road angling

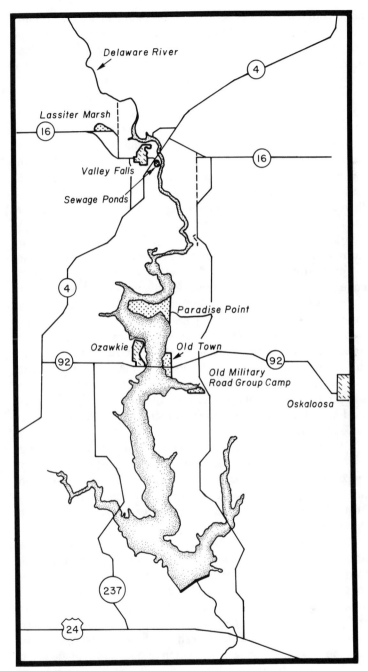

MAP 10. *Perry Lake*

off to your left provides access to additional marsh habitat. Entry into this area is prohibited from 1 October through 15 January, but at other times you can park and walk down to bird these marshes. If it is not too wet, you can continue along this road as it traverses marshy areas on both sides but watch out for muddy stretches and deep ruts. In 1.8 miles from the turn-off this road comes to a stop sign at K16. (If this road is too wet to travel, you can get to K16 on the hardtop.) In either case, turn left and follow K16 into Valley Falls. Just after crossing the Delaware River, K16 turns right (west). At this point you might pull off and check the Valley Falls sewage ponds and wetlands along the river for gulls and other waterbirds. Continue west on K16 for 1.6 miles and then turn right to reach another series of marshes developed in the Perry Wildlife Management Area.

After crossing a bridge about 0.5 mile from K16 the hardtop turns left, but you should continue straight on a gravel road for 1.3 miles from K16 where it dead-ends in a parking area at the edge of the riparian vegetation along the Delaware River. Get out and walk to your left (west) through a grassland area to inspect the pond and marsh. During passerine migration it would also be worthwhile to spend some time searching for warblers and other songbirds in the trees along the river. Return to the hard-top, turn right, and proceed about 0.4 mile to reach Lassiter Marsh which extends for about the next half mile along the road and provides excellent opportunities for viewing waterfowl. This road soon intersects K16 where you should turn left and return to Valley Falls.

If your time is limited and you would just like to survey Perry Lake for waterfowl, you can reach a good point of observation by continuing west on K92 for just 1 mile past the turn-off mentioned above for Paradise Point and the marshes. At this point turn left (south) into the Old Town Recreation Area for access to the lakeshore.

Explore an upland oak-hickory area nearby for additional variety on your bird list. From that point on K92 where you would turn north towards the Paradise Point road, turn left (south) and continue for 1.3 miles to reach the entrance into the Old Military Road Group Campground. Camping here is only by reservation, but you can walk in unannounced by either taking the Perry Lake Trail that follows the lakeshore or just walking the road past the barrier. In fact, a combination of both will provide access to a variety of habitats. Leave your car in the parking area just before the road barrier and take the Perry Lake Trail through both a hillside of young oak, hickory, and elm with a few scattered older trees and a more open area with cedars and remnant prairie grasses, until you come to the entrance road in less than a mile. Leave the trail at this point and follow the road into more mature oak-hickory forest to reach the Carbine group camping area. From the amphitheater in this campground, take a trail downhill to intersect the Perry Lake Trail, and follow the lake trail to your right, back to the parking area. During the breeding season you should find both Red-eyed and Yellow-throated Vireos as well as Summer Tanagers and other species characteristic of the upland deciduous forest community, while Louisiana Waterthrushes and Kentucky Warblers can be expected in the creek valleys. Both Whip-poor-wills and Chuck-will's-widows can be heard calling on spring and summer nights.

Oskaloosa,
Kansas

_____

_____

Forest-Prairie
Mosaic

The watershed of Big Bull Creek drains south through the forest-prairie mosaic of eastern Kansas. Although most of the prairie has been converted into cropland and tame pastures, patches of upland oak-hickory forest remain. Hillsdale Lake, formed in the valley of Big Bull Creek, provides an excellent mix of aquatic and terrestrial habitats that attract a variety of birds throughout the year, including large numbers of waterfowl during spring and fall migrations.

Drive north on U.S. 169 from the junction with K68 near Paola for 3 miles and exit west toward the town of Hillsdale on 255th Street. Continue west through Hillsdale for 2.7 miles and turn right on a gravel road to make a circuit of the lake that will allow you to sample the variety of area habitats. If you would like a map of the area, continue west on 255th Street for about 0.5 mile to reach the visitor center. If the weather has been wet, ask about road conditions in the area of the lake as well, since this tour will take you on some dirt roads before you have completed it.

Continue north and then west on the gravel road for 3.6 miles from the 255th Street turn-off. Then turn left (south) onto a dirt road. If the road is impassable, you could park here and walk the rest of the way; it is not far. At 0.5 mile you come to a crossroad; turn right and continue for 0.3 mile and park at a turn-off to your right. On the north side of the road, just beyond where you are parked, is a mature oak-hickory forest in which such characteristic species as Yellow-throated Vireo, Louisiana Waterthrush, Kentucky Warbler, and Summer Tanager nest. On the south side of the road the vegetation is more open with a scattered stand of elm and honey locust and the expected edge species of birds. This particular stopping place should be excellent during migration because of the variety of habitats in the immediate vicinity, but it is also worth visiting in winter for the mixed species flocks of forest birds as well as the variety of sparrows in the edge habitats.

Retrace your route to the dirt road and turn right to proceed south again. The road dead-ends in 0.7 mile, providing an excellent spot to scan the open water of both arms of the lake for waterfowl. To the southwest in the dead trees flooded by the western arm of the lake is a Great Blue Heron heronry to which the birds return in April.

Return to the gravel road and turn left (west), continuing to follow the road as it turns right, and then turn left at the next crossroad, about 2 miles from the point where you returned to the gravel. At a little over 0.5 mile from this corner, the road crosses a creek. Park here and walk down the west side of the creek to reach a relatively open stand of elm and honey locust with some hackberry and hickory; this is best during the periods of passerine migration. If you continue far enough, you reach the shore of an inlet from the lake. The east side of the creek, also bordered by an excellent stand of hardwoods, is good for Brown Creepers in the winter and nuthatches and woodpeckers throughout the year.

In about 2 miles from this creek the road crosses the inlet of Big Bull Creek which offers shallow water habitat suitable for waterfowl and waders. Beyond this bridge the road turns south and crosses the inlet of Rock Creek in about 1.5 miles. It is similarly worthwhile to stop here and scan the shallow waters for waders, especially concentrations of shorebirds. From the bridge over Rock Creek, look west up Rock Creek. A Great Blue Heron colony of about fifty nests is in trees on the west edge of an open field. After crossing Rock Creek, the road (Crescent Hill Road) jogs left and then right. Then turn left (east) at the next crossroad (247th Street), proceed 1 mile east, and follow the road as it turns south as Waverly Road. In 1 mile you will reach a bridge over Wade Branch. Stop the car here and scan the water and shoreline for waterfowl and shorebirds, depending upon the season. Continue south on Waverly Road; about 1.8 miles from the bridge, turn left (east) on 271st Street. In approximately 1 mile you will reach a hardtop road; turn left and continue across the dam and past the visitor center on the east side of the dam, reaching the crossroad where you first started this tour. The entire circuit of the lake is about 18 miles.

Together, Big Hill Lake, a U.S. Army Corps of Engineers reservoir, and the adjacent Big Hill Wildlife Management Area, administered by the Kansas Department of Wildlife and Parks, provide a variety of habitats that offer the birder good opportunities from April through early October. To reach this area, drive west out of Parsons on U.S. 160. At the junction with K133, which goes north to Dennis, you should turn south (left) on a hard-surfaced road that brings you to the Big Hill Wildlife Management Area, a rolling landscape of open pastures and tree-dotted valleys. The hedgerows of persimmon, osage orange, redbud, and dogwood provide nesting habitat for Northern Bobwhite, Blue Grosbeak, Orchard Oriole, Bell's Vireo, and Scissor-tailed Flycatcher. In the fall, there will be many American Tree Sparrows as well as Song, White-crowned, and Harris' Sparrows.

To reach Big Hill Lake continue on the hardtop road to the Timber Hill Recreation Area. If you follow the signs to the boat launching ramp, you will be afforded a good view of the northern part of the lake. The oak-hickory woods on Timber Hill offer an assemblage of woodpeckers, Blue Jays, and the usual mix of chickadees and nuthatches during most of the year, except in the most severe winters. If you visit here at dawn or dusk in the breeding season, you may be treated to a chorus of both Chuck-will's-widows and Whip-poor-wills.

Return to the main road and continue south, following the signs to the Mound Valley and Cherryvale Recreation Areas. The southeastern portion of the lake can be scanned from the boat ramp at Mound Valley, but if you continue another 2 miles, past the dam, you can view the lake from the boat ramp in the Cherryvale Area. If you walk the woods in this area during the early summer, you should be able to find Carolina and Bewick's Wrens, Black-and-white and Kentucky Warblers, Ovenbirds, and American Redstarts.

PLEASANTON, KANSAS

This tour is rewarding at any season, and your species list will be diverse because of the variety of habitats you encounter. Drive on U.S. 69 approximately 12 miles north of Pleasanton and exit east at K152 to reach La Cygne Lake, a large cooling water lake for a coal-fired electric generating plant. Continue for 0.3 mile to the first road on your left and turn here, continuing for about 2 miles to the entrance of the Linn County Park (entrance fee required) on your right. Turn left on the first road beyond park headquarters. This road winds through an upland of oak-hickory which can be checked in the evening for Barred Owls, Eastern Screech-owls, and Woodcocks in April and May. Continue on this road through the camping area to the marina and boat ramp at the next right, which provides an excellent vantage point for viewing the lake for waterfowl. Among the species expected here during migration and winter are both Eared and Horned Grebes, scoters, and all three species of mergansers as well as many gulls and the more common species of ducks and geese. Return to the main park road and turn right to reach another boat ramp and vantage point at the north end of the lake. To obtain viewing access for the lake near the dam, leave the county park and return to the eastern extension of K152, turn left, proceed for 0.7 mile, and park along the side of the road. At this point you can walk through an opening in the fence to reach the edge of the lake and view the southern end. Since this is probably the best spot on the lake for seeing the greatest variety of waterfowl, check it carefully.

Although the Marais des Cygnes Wildlife Management Area can be entered more directly by returning to U.S. 69 and going south toward Pleasanton for about 4 miles, you can follow a route with more habitat diversity by turning around and returning to the place where the road to Linn County Park turned off. This time turn left (south), continue for 0.4 mile and then turn left (east), again on the dirt road. This road, through a wet meadow below the dam, is good for Horned Larks and occasionally longspurs in winter, Vesper Sparrows and other migrant sparrows in spring, and Lark Sparrows in summer. In about 1

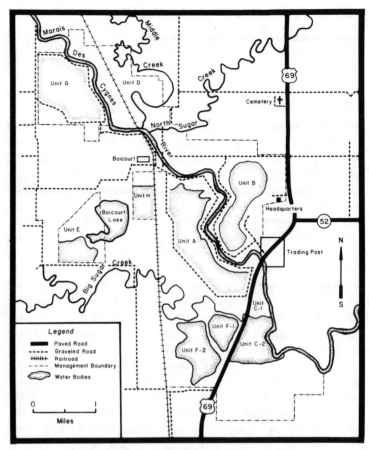

MAP 11. *Marais des Cygnes Wildlife Management Area*

mile this road turns south. One mile beyond this corner there is a side road to the right and beyond this road a bridge. In spring and during the nesting season it would be worthwhile to stop the car here and walk along the road to explore the woods on either side of the road, but remember this is private land so stay on the road. Cerulean Warbler has nested here, and Louisiana Waterthrush and Barred Owl can be found along the stream. Then take the side road east for 1 mile to reach u.s. 69. Turn left and go south for 2.5 miles; then turn right and stop immediately at the small cemetery on your left which might harbor Scissor-tailed Flycatchers. This road continues for the first half mile through open fields. Occasionally stop the car and check the taller dead trees across the field to your right (north) for Red-shouldered Hawks, a relatively common permanent resident here. The road continues into more scrubby growth; be alert for nesting White-eyed Vireos and American Woodcock on the south side of the road near the gas pipeline valve. Both sides of the road soon become forested with a well-developed under-story. This can be an outstanding spot in the spring if your presence happens to coincide with a good warbler flight, but even if the flight has been poor or you are here in the summer, time spent in this area can be rewarding. At 1.3 miles from u.s. 69 you come to a bridge over North Sugar Creek. This is the best area to stop the car and explore. Nesting species that can be seen here include Wood Duck, Red-shouldered Hawk, Barred Owl, Pileated Woodpecker, Acadian Flycatcher, Tufted Titmouse, White-breasted Nuthatch, Carolina Wren, Wood Thrush, Blue-gray Gnatcatcher, Yellow-throated Vireo, Red-eyed Vireo, Warbling Vireo, Prothonotary Warbler, Northern Parula, Cerulean Warbler, Kentucky Warbler, and Summer Tanager. Other nesting possibilities include Black-and-white Warbler, American Red-start, and Scarlet Tanager. About 100 yards east of the bridge a field access lane goes north along the east side of the creek, on which birding can be especially fine. Of course, this area is also good for passerines during fall migration.

At the next intersection, 0.5 mile beyond the bridge, turn left and stop the car. It is often productive to explore the west continuation of the road you were just driving, but you must walk this unimproved dirt road. This road enters Unit D of the Marais des Cygnes Wildlife Management Area soon after crossing Sugar Creek, which you must ford. The road continues through riparian hardwood forest, and once you enter the refuge you can spend some effort searching for birds off the road. In the spring the water table is high so you might get wet, but this is one of the best places to discover Yellow-crowned Night-herons which nest in this part of the refuge. Of course, you can expect to see many of the species mentioned above in this excellent site for migrant and nesting passerines.

Return to the car and continue for just a short distance to the point where the road turns right, 2.1 miles from u.s. 69. Stop the car here and check the pond on the right for shorebirds, herons, and waterfowl. The woods on your left are on private land, but this is a particularly good spot to find Yellow-throated Vireos along the road. This road makes a left turn and then right and left turns, crosses North Sugar Creek, and then makes another left turn to the east. Continue east for about 1 mile, then turn right at the first opportunity into Unit B of the refuge. If this entrance is closed, continue east for 1 mile to u.s. 69; then turn right (south), reaching Trading Post in about 2 miles. This intersection is a good place to stop and listen for Wood Thrush and in the evening for Chuck-will's-widows. The road continues through forest for a short distance and then passes an oxbow extension of the Unit B pool. Check here for Green-backed Herons and Wood Ducks as well as migrant passerines. The road continues along the riparian forest bordering the Marais des Cygnes River. Stop from time to time and check these woods for Acadian Flycatchers and Louisiana Waterthrushes during the breeding season and a variety of passerines during migration. As you continue, the open water of the refuge pool will become more accessible on your left. The cattails along the border of this pool should be searched during migration for American Bitterns, Soras, and Virginia Rails. Continue to follow this road as it turns east around the south side of refuge pool B. Just before the road goes up a slight grade into the woods, park the car and spend some time searching the riparian forest along the river for Northern Parulas and Cerulean and Prothonotary Warblers. In the evening, both Chuck-will's-widows and Whip-poor-wills can be heard from this spot. If you have the time, it would be worthwhile to walk east on the road, up the hill, and then follow the road to the left which continues through the oak-hickory forest to a dead end. Summer Tanagers nest here, and occasionally Scarlet Tanagers as well. Return to the car, drive up the hill, but turn right. In 0.3 mile you will intersect u.s. 69 at the town of Trading Post.

Turn right (south) on u.s. 69, continue across the bridge over the Marais des Cygnes River for 0.2 mile to the Boicourt Road and turn right. Immediately after this turn, take the first road to your left to follow around the south and west sides of the pool in Unit A. This largest pool on the refuge is excellent for herons, including egrets, in summer and for waterfowl, especially Snow Geese, as well as Rough-legged Hawks and Bald Eagles in winter. In spring and fall there are often large numbers of American White Pelicans and Double-crested Cormorants, Ring-billed Gulls, Black Terns, a few Caspian Terns, and occasionally a Common Tern with the Forster's Terns. If the water level is low, shorebirds can be found along the margins of the pool; and in late April, Palm Warblers can also be found along the water's edge, especially on the north side of the pool. At 3.4 miles from U.S. 69 you come to a "T." Turn left toward the little town of Boicourt; at 0.2 mile, just before the railroad tracks, turn right towards Unit G. After 0.7 mile from this corner you pass under the railroad. At the first available space along the road, park the car and explore the riparian forest along the Marais des Cygnes River to your right as well as the slope forest on your left. In addition to the many species already mentioned for this location, this particular spot has the highest probability for the Yellow-throated Warbler. Continue on this road until it turns right (north). This is another good place to stop. Follow a trail off the road to the left (west) for a short distance and listen for Wood Thrush, Carolina Wren, Acadian Flycatcher, and Louisiana Waterthrush.

In a few tenths of a mile you will come to Unit G. Turn left (west) and check the marsh on your left for Wood Duck and Prothonotary Warblers. Scan the dead trees in this pool for nesting Tree Swallows and for Ospreys in spring and fall. Continue west on the dike road as it enters a forested area and proceed up the side of a wooded slope. Characteristic species of upland oak-hickory can be found here: Red-eyed Vireo, Wood Thrush, and Summer Tanager. Eastern Screech-owls will often respond to taped calls along this road. A road enters from your left soon after the road you are on turns. In 0.7 mile, turn right to continue along the north side of the pool in Unit G. Although dependent upon water level, the northern and eastern sides of the pool provide the best shorebird habitat, birds sometimes occurring in the hundreds with Lesser Golden Plover, Short-billed Dowitcher, and even Buff-breasted Sandpiper present along with the more common species. Also listen for Willow Flycatchers nesting on this stretch of the road in late spring and early summer. This road will bring you back to the point where you entered Unit G.

Turn left and follow the road back to Boicourt; turn left and then continue straight along the east side of Unit A until you again reach U.S. 69. Unit G may be closed in winter.

Turn right (south) onto U.S. 69. On the east side of the highway there are two pools. The northern is used primarily as a refuge during the waterfowl season, but at other times of the year it also attracts waterfowl, herons, and shorebirds. Northern Shovelers have nested here. The southern pool on the east side of the highway is prime shorebird habitat since water levels are often low. White-rumped Sandpipers sometimes occur in large numbers during May, and Hudsonian Godwits can occasionally be found earlier in the spring. The shoulders along U.S. 69 are wide enough to provide ample space to pull off. To check the pools on the west side of the highway, pull off to your right into a parking area 0.9 mile south of the Boicourt Road. This pool often has large numbers of diving ducks, and the wet, grassy areas on the west side of this pool are frequented by rails and Marsh Wrens during migration. The west side of this pool as well as access to the southern pool on the west side of the highway can be obtained by turning into a parking area off to the right of U.S. 69, 1.5 miles south of the Boicourt Road. From this point, Pleasanton is approximately 3.5 miles south on U.S. 69.

Pleasanton is also the starting point to tour the Dingus Natural Area, a Nature Conservancy site administered by the Kansas Ornithological Society. Proceed south about 2 miles on U.S. 69 from Pleasanton and turn right (west) on K52. Continue through the town of Mound City and then turn right onto a gravel road, 9.3 miles from U.S. 69, just at the top of the hill. At 1.4 miles from this turn-off the road makes a left turn to the west, and at 2.2 miles from the turn-off the Dingus Natural Area will be on your right. There is a sign at the southeast corner of the property, and the property extends 0.5 mile to the west and to Little Sugar Creek on the north. There is no boundary fence, and there are no trails through the area. Care should be taken to minimize your disturbance of the vegetation. This is an excellent stand of mature oak-hickory in the uplands and riparian forest along Little Sugar Creek. In spring and summer the evening chorus of Barred Owls, Chuck-will's-widows, and Whip-poor-wills is almost overpowering. Passerine migration can be excellent, while nesting species of note include Northern Parula, Ovenbird, Kentucky Warbler, Summer Tanager, and possibly Scarlet Tanager and Worm-eating Warbler.

SENECA, KANSAS

One of the most westerly stands of upland oak-hickory forest is at Nemaha County State Lake in the southwest corner of the wildlife area. To reach this site take κ63 south from its junction with u.s. 36 just east of Seneca for 5.5 miles and then turn left into the Nemaha Wildlife Management Area. Follow the roads through this area, stopping from time to time to explore the rather extensively developed forest on the slopes above the lake. Expected breeding species include Eastern Wood-pewee, Great Crested Flycatcher, Tufted Titmouse, Wood Thrush, Red-eyed Vireo, Summer Tanager, Rose-breasted Grosbeak, and Indigo Bunting.

84

Forest-Prairie
Mosaic

This area in the northwestern corner of Clay County provides such a variety of habitats that it is worth visiting any time of the year, although the period from April through October offers the birder the longest species list. To reach Smithville, drive north on U.S. 169 from downtown Kansas City for 18 miles. After crossing M92, continue for 1 mile and turn right (east) on County Road DD and go an additional mile to reach the visitors' center at Smithville Lake, a U.S. Army Corps of Engineers impoundment, where you can obtain a map of the area.

From the headquarters area, cross the dam and drive north on Route F. At the intersection with County Road W, turn right (east) and follow the hardtop as it makes a gentle turn south to reach the town of Paradise. Leave Route W at this point, going south on another hardtop road to reach the Camp Branch Bridge Area, one of the better locations to check the lake for waterfowl. One of the main attractions of Smithville Lake is its resident flock of the Giant Canada Goose. During migration and in the winter, this largest subspecies contrasts sharply with the middle-sized and small races also present. In addition, you should expect to see a good variety of puddle and diving ducks on the lake during these periods.

Return to Route W and turn right to continue east again for 2 miles to reach the entrance to the Trimble Wildlife Area. This is a great place for bird watching. In the breeding season, American and Least Bitterns can be found in the marshes, and you can expect to see Great Blue and Little Blue Herons, Yellow-crowned and Black-crowned Night-herons, and Green-backed Herons. With a little patience, you might also see several species of rails. This is one of the few locations within the area of this guide where you can expect to discover nesting Song Sparrows. If you walk along the willows that border the marsh you can find Willow Flycatchers and Yellow Warblers and hear Sedge Wrens singing in the weedy areas.

When you leave this area to return to Route W, turn east again, go just about a quarter mile, and turn left on a gravel road. At 2 miles north of the hardtop, this road turns left (west). Just 0.4 mile beyond this corner another gravel road runs due south; follow this road to an excellent stand of upland oak-hickory forest in the northern portion of the Trimble Wildlife Area. The woods in this part of the park are very good for owls; Eastern Screech-owl and Great Horned and Barred Owls can be located with little difficulty. During the breeding season you will find Yellow-billed Cuckoo, Great Crested Flycatcher, Eastern Wood-pewee, Wood Thrush, Blue-gray Gnatcatcher, Red-eyed and Warbling Vireos, Kentucky Warbler, and Rose-breasted Grosbeak. Both Summer and Scarlet Tanagers are possible nesting species as well. Walk south through the woods towards the lake. The forest becomes more open, and you might add Eastern Phoebe, Eastern King-bird, Eastern Bluebird, and Yellow-throated Vireo to your list. A few Cedar Waxwings nest in this area from time to time. When you reach the lake, listen for the loud "tweet-tweet-tweet" of the Prothonotary Warbler from the dead trees along the shore. In fall, winter, and early spring, it is not too unusual to flush a Short-eared Owl from along the water's edge.

To continue your tour of Smithville Lake, return to the gravel road you were on after leaving Route w and turn left (west) to County Road j. If you turn left on Route j, you will intersect Route w in about 1.5 miles. If you turn right on Route j you will come to a "T" with Route c where you should turn left (north) to reach Plattsburg MO. As you drive on Routes j and c through this rolling farm country, be sure to watch the fenceposts during the breeding season for Upland Sandpipers. If you stop at mead-ows and fallow fields along the way, you will probably hear Field Sparrows, Grasshopper Sparrows, and Dickcissels, and per-haps, a Bobolink. Both Eastern and Western Meadowlarks occur here. In the winter, watch for Northern Harriers and Rough-legged Hawks.

At Plattsburg there are a number of public access areas to the northern reaches of the lake and the flooded river channel. In the breeding season you will find White-breasted Nuthatch, Car-olina Wren, Northern Parula, American Redstart, Rufous-sided Towhee, and other species characteristic of the riparian forest of this region. Keep alert as well for hen Wood Ducks and their broods during early summer. From Plattsburg, go west on M116 to reach u.s. 169 in about 6 miles.

ST. PAUL, KANSAS

*Forest-Prairie
Mosaic*

The major attraction of the Neosho Wildlife Management Area, located in the broad, flat floodplain of the Neosho River, is the population of migrant and wintering ducks that stays here to take advantage of the food and open water provided by the four pools in the refuge. If you visit in summer, however, you will not be disappointed. Wood Ducks nest here; and if water levels are satisfactory, you may well see good numbers of herons and egrets. Both Yellow-crowned and Black-crowned Night-herons have nested on the area, and Great Blue, Little Blue, and Green-backed Herons and Snowy and Great Egrets will be seen occasionally.

Start your tour in St. Paul and go east on K57. Just beyond the rest area at the edge of town on the south side of the road, turn right on a gravel road and drive 1 mile along the edge of the wildlife area to the site of a bridge over the Neosho River (the road no longer goes over the bridge). Stop here at any time of year to listen for Pileated Woodpeckers and Carolina Wrens. In spring and summer, you should take the trail along the river to find Yellow-throated Vireos, Prothonotary Warblers, Kentucky Warblers, and Northern Parulas that nest in this stand of timber. A visit at dusk during late March and April could be rewarded with displaying American Woodcocks.

Return to K57, turn right, and drive 1 mile east to reach the entrance to the refuge on the south side of the highway. The refuge is small, and a system of graveled roadways along the pools makes the area quite accessible to the visitor interested in seeing birds. There are many Mallards both in migration and during the winter, but you will also see good numbers of Green-winged Teal, Blue-winged Teal, Northern Pintail, American Wigeon, Northern Shoveler, Gadwall, and a few diving ducks.

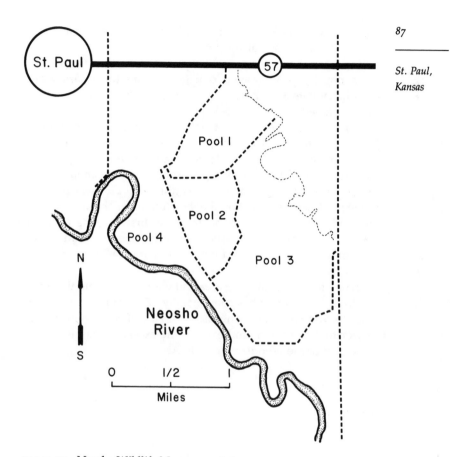

MAP 12. *Neosho Wildlife Management Area*

88

Forest-Prairie
Mosaic

Woodson County State Fishing Lake and Wildlife Management Area is a microcosm of the forest-prairie mosaic, affording the bird watcher the opportunity to experience excellent upland tallgrass prairie, good upland oak forest, and the riparian and aquatic habitats associated with a delightful little lake formed in the watershed of Sandy Creek.

To reach this site, go west on U.S. 54 for 7.5 miles from its junction with U.S. 75 in Yates Center and turn left (south) just before the highway goes under a railroad grade crossing. At 0.3 mile from this turn, turn left again and proceed for about 3 miles to a stop sign. Turn left here, and continue for 1.4 miles to a fork in the road, where you should bear left to enter the area. Follow the road to your right around the lake, first crossing over the dam and spillway. On the east side of the lake, the road passes through a nice stand of red oak forest with blackjack and post oak in the uplands. As the road continues you come into more open habitat in the camping area and then loop around the north end of the lake which has good marshy vegetation along its margins. As you continue along the west side of the lake, it would be worthwhile to park and explore the excellent prairie to your right, part of the Woodson Wildlife Area.

OAK-HICKORY FOREST AND RIPARIAN FOREST

ATCHISON, KANSAS

Two upland sites on the Kansas side of the Missouri River are representative of the oak-hickory forest. To reach Atchison County State Fishing Lake, take K7 north out of Atchison. At 5.8 miles from the junction of K7 and u.s. 73 in Atchison, turn left (west) on a gravel road and continue for 2 miles, and then turn right and go north for 0.5 mile to the entrance of the park. The best habitat is reached by turning left along the south side of the lake all the way to the end of the road. Park here and enter the riparian forest along the stream flowing into the lake at this point. As you walk uphill, the riparian forest merges with an oak, hickory, and linden forest. Nesting species include both Chuck-will's-widows and Whip-poor-wills, Blue-gray Gnatcatchers, Red-eyed and Yellow-throated Vireos, Kentucky Warbler, Northern Parula, and Summer Tanager. The forested slope south of road is also good, but not very extensive.

Reach Atchison County Park by taking u.s. 73 west out of Atchison towards Lancaster. At 5.4 miles beyond Lancaster, turn left (west) at the town of Huron. In 3.3 miles the hardtop turns right, but continue straight ahead on the gravel for another mile; then turn left and enter the park by a right turn through the gate. The best birding is in the riparian thickets of willow, elm, locust, box elder, and silver maple along creek drainages entering the lake on the east end and along the south shore. None of these, however, is very extensive so the site is good for the migration period, but breeding bird diversity is low. The upland areas comprise open, park-like stands of bur oak which attract a limited variety of migrants.

To explore riparian habitats east of Atchison along the Missouri River, take u.s. 59 east across the river into Missouri, then turn right on M45, and go south for 1 mile to the junction with M138. Turn right here, and go west for 1 mile to reach Lewis and Clark State Park and Lake. The state park contains both good ponds for migrant waterfowl and waders and the eastern arm of Sugar Lake (see Kansas City MO). In April and October you will find a variety of puddle ducks, especially Green-winged and Blue-winged Teals, but many Mallards, Gadwalls, Northern Pintails, American Wigeons, and Northern Shovelers will also

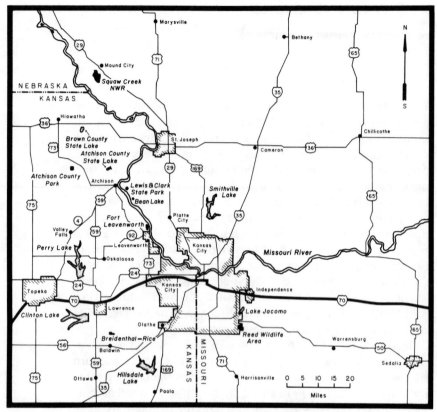

MAP 13. *Oak-Hickory Forest and Northern Forest-Prairie Mosaic*

round out your list. Although diving ducks are less common, you can expect large flocks of all three species of geese, including both morphs of the Snow Goose. In late summer and early fall, depending on the water level, the ponds attract the expected variety of sandpipers and small numbers of Semipalmated Plovers. During the summer in the cottonwoods around Sugar Lake there will be Warbling Vireos, Yellow Warblers, many Eastern Kingbirds, and Northern (Baltimore) Orioles.

Atchison,
Kansas

*Oak-Hickory
Forest and
Riparian Forest*

One of finest examples of intact upland oak-hickory forest is preserved by the Nature Conservancy at its Breidenthal Biological Reserve north of Baldwin City (contact the Division of Biological Sciences, University of Kansas, Lawrence KS 66045, for permission to enter). This excellent stand of forest, composed of white, red, and black oak, shagbark hickory, and green ash, is dissected by numerous stream branches with chinquapin oak on the drier ridges. A visit during any season of the year will provide you with a list of species characteristic of the habitat, but fall and spring migrations are especially good because of this habitat's attraction to species of thrushes, vireos, and warblers seldom seen any farther west in Kansas. Species present during the breeding season include Whip-poor-will and Chuck-will's-widow, Wood Thrush, Yellow-throated Vireo, Northern Parula, Louisiana Waterthrush, Summer Tanager, Rose-breasted Grosbeak, and sometimes Scarlet Tanager.

To reach the reserve, take Douglas Co. 1055 north out of Baldwin City for 2 miles beyond the intersection with U.S. 56. Just before you get to the turn-off, the road will curve right over a hill. The turn-off is on the downhill side to your left. There is a small parking space at the entrance gate, open to pedestrian traffic. Park here and walk in, but stay on the trails to minimize your impact on the forest floor.

Just to the east across Douglas Co. 1055 is the Rice Biological Reserve, similar in habitat except for a greater amount of edge adjacent to an old field on the north side. You are also permitted to wander more freely in your search for birds at this site since it has not been specifically dedicated for research and thus there is little chance you would inadvertently interfere with on-going projects. From the parking space at the Breidenthal tract continue north on Douglas Co. 1055 for 0.1 mile and turn right (east) on a gravel road that goes along the north edge of the Rice Biological Reserve. At 0.3 miles from the corner you will come to a bridge; just before the bridge there is space along the road on your right to pull off and park so that you can explore the area on foot. An alternate approach is to continue for 0.2 mile to the next crossroad at the northeast corner of the tract. Turn right here, park, and enter the area at this point.

INDEPENDENCE, MISSOURI

The cottonwoods and willows along the south shore of the Missouri River at La Benite Park are a continuation of the unfortunately frequently interrupted corridor of riparian vegetation along the river that many species use as an avenue for their migratory flights in the fall and spring. If you happen to be there at the most opportune time, the trees will almost "drip" migrant birds. During the breeding season, you can expect the characteristic set of riparian species—Red-eyed and Warbling Vireos, Yellow Warbler, Common Yellowthroat, and American Redstart. From early May to September you can find both Northern (Baltimore) and Orchard Orioles nesting here, using the "cotton" from the trees to line their nests. In fall and winter, there are flocks of Harris' and White-crowned Sparrows in the brushy patches along the river, and you have a good chance of finding a Winter Wren.

To reach La Benite Park take I-70, M78, or U.S. 24 east through Independence until you intersect M291. Go north on M291 towards Liberty MO, but just before you cross the Missouri River exit east into the park. Park and walk the trails along the river.

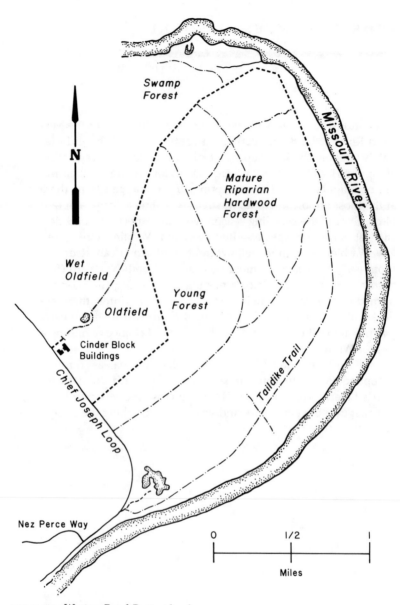

Swamp
Forest

N

Missouri River

Mature
Riparian
Hardwood
Forest

Wet
Oldfield

Oldfield

Young
Forest

Cinder Block
Buildings

Chief Joseph Loop

Taildike Trail

Nez Perce Way

0   1/2   1

Miles

MAP 14. *Weston Bend Bottomland*

LEAVENWORTH, KANSAS

Colonel Henry Leavenworth established an army post near the present site of this town in northeastern Kansas in 1827 at the gateway for western expansion on the Oregon and Sante Fe trails. Since 1881 it has been the home of the U.S. Army Command and General Staff College. There probably is no better example of mature riparian forest in the whole region of this guide than that located in the bottomlands of Weston Bend on Fort Leavenworth. Some of the trees in this stand of elm, cottonwood, hackberry, pecan, walnut, and sycamore were alive when Lewis and Clark passed this way on their exploratory trip up the Missouri River. What makes this site even more attractive to the birder is the variety of habitats adjacent to the forest—younger stands of forest trees, old fields managed by the Forestry Department on the post to stay in relatively early seral stages, and small lakes and water-filled ditches. Any season is excellent, although the rank growth of nettles and the legions of mosquitoes make summertime birding in the forest an adventure in perseverance.

To reach the bottomlands, take U.S. 73/K7 (4th Street) north through Leavenworth; 0.7 mile beyond Shawnee Street near the center of town, the routes turn left. Get into the right lane after making this turn since in 0.2 mile you will turn right through the gates of Fort Leavenworth onto Grant Avenue. Fort Leavenworth is an open post and encourages visitors since it is an important historic site; be sure to observe the speed limits and watch out for pedestrians. When you get to the statue of General Grant, 1.4 miles from the entrance, bear right. On your left will be the imposing walls of the U.S. Disciplinary Barracks. Instead of turning left in front of this prison, continue straight on Riverside Avenue as it curves to the right downhill for 0.2 mile and then turn left on Chief Joseph Loop. Cross over the railroad tracks and continue straight ahead on Nez Perce Way, past the picnic grounds to where you again intersect Chief Joseph Loop on the top of the levee. You will note that traffic is one-way. Turn left on the levee, continue with the Missouri River on your right for 0.2 mile from the corner, and park along the edge of the road where there is sufficient shoulder.

There are two trails off to your right. The closer one goes only a short distance to a small lake. The one closer to the Missouri River (the taildike trail) can be followed all the way around Weston Bend, eventually bringing you back after several miles to the buildings you see about 1 mile down the levee road. If you choose to walk this route, be sure to take the side trails off to your left that provide access into the parts of the forest older than those along the border of the river. In the breeding season the older areas of the forest will have Acadian Flycatchers, American Redstarts, and Scarlet Tanagers. Any time of the year, you might find a Pileated Woodpecker. During migration, however, the edge vegetation along this taildike trail provides the best opportunity for vireos and warblers.

On another road off Chief Joseph Loop, just 0.4 mile farther down the levee, you can park and then follow on foot. This trail also provides exceptional bird watching as it goes along a man-made slough that is usually filled with water and attracts a variety of birds, including herons. As you continue down this road, the cottonwoods, elms, and ashes on your left are younger since this side was open field as late as 1965. In addition to such species as Northern Cardinal, Rufous-sided Towhee, Rose-breasted Grosbeak, and Black-capped Chickadee, watch for Wild Turkey in this younger but thicker growth. The trees on your right are much older, and some of the massive sycamores support a colony of nesting Great Blue Herons. As you walk along the edge of the older woods, listen for the Wood Thrushes nesting here. This trail eventually intersects the taildike trail where you can turn right to go towards the river or left to go back towards Chief Joseph Loop.

Just 0.2 mile farther along the levee another road to your right is better surfaced and can be driven, except in wet weather. For 0.8 mile it skirts an old field, a summer nesting habitat for Dickcissel, Common Yellowthroat, and Red-winged Blackbird with Sedge Wren and American Woodcock in the damper spots; in winter there are usually large flocks of mixed sparrows, including Swamp Sparrows. This road then intersects the taildike trail. You can drive the dike for a short distance by turning right, but it is better to park and walk. On your left is a lower area of younger forest, which in 1940 was a swamp but which has since silted in to permit the growth of larger trees. Given the number of natural sloughs through this stand, it is an excellent site for nesting Prothonotary Warblers and Wood Duck, and Pileated Woodpeckers are to be expected here all year long. On your right the mature floodplain forest can be explored along several side trails that branch off the dike trail.

There is one last road off Chief Joseph Loop, just beyond the cinder block buildings on your right. Turn here and park, since the road ends almost immediately. Walk this trail toward the woods and around a small lake. To your left a wet oldfield habitat is usually a good place to find Willow Flycatchers; on your right is the old field described above.

To return to the main entrance, continue on Chief Joseph Loop around the airfield, giving the right-of-way to low-flying aircraft, turn right just past the skeet range, cross the railroad, and turn left. Continue across Sheridan Drive to Sylvan Trail and go up the hill west of the Disciplinary Barracks and turn left on McPherson. Then turn right on McClellan, go past the Main Parade Ground (the original center of the post), turn left on Kearney, and then right on Grant Avenue at the general's statue. From here it is about 1.4 miles to the entrance on U.S. 73/K7.

———————————

—————

*Oak-Hickory
Forest and
Riparian Forest*

Although the Squaw Creek National Wildlife Refuge provides extensive marsh habitat for nesting Least Bitterns, King and Virginia Rails, Soras, Marsh Wrens, and Yellow-headed Blackbirds, migration periods as well as early winter are the best times to visit this site. The main pools on the refuge provide loitering space for huge concentrations of Snow, Canada, and Greater White-fronted Geese as well as impressive numbers of puddle ducks. At times, goose populations can exceed half a million birds. Scattered among the tens of thousands of Snow Geese, small numbers of Ross' Geese are often worth your patience to discover. From late November through the winter, visitors will also see Bald Eagles in the dead trees adjacent to the pools or on the ice, feeding on dead waterfowl. During peak periods more than one hundred eagles can be on the refuge. During the shorebird migration, check mud flats for waders. Especially numerous are Pectoral and White-rumped Sandpipers, Long-billed Dowitchers, and Wilson's Phalaropes. During late April and May, you should expect relatively large flocks of Hudsonian Godwits, while in August and early September you should search the drier areas of the mud flats around the main pools for Buff-breasted Sandpipers.

To reach the refuge, take I-29 southeast from Mound City for 5 miles and exit on U.S. 159 (exit 79) toward Rulo NE. Follow the signs for 2 miles to reach refuge headquarters where you can obtain a map of the area and a bird checklist. While in the headquarters area, take the trail to the observation shelter on the loess bluffs; this provides an unobstructed view of the entire refuge area. The panorama across a sky filled with thousands of waterfowl is nothing short of spectacular. During passerine migration, the woods on the bluffs are worth checking, and at any season you may find Eastern Screech-owls, Great Horned Owls, or Barred Owls here. In winter, check the cedars very carefully for Northern Saw-whet Owls.

The best way to tour the refuge is driving the 10-mile perimeter road that circles the pools; allow about 3.5 hours to adequately complete the tour. After leaving headquarters, take the

*Long before we were here to mark their presence, Bald Eagles came down to
winter in the cottonwoods along the rivers. With the construction of
numerous reservoirs and the protection afforded by an aware public, eagles
can readily be found throughout the region from November to April.*

refuge road west towards the main pool. Then turn left (south)
and follow the dike road along the southeastern, southwestern,
northwestern, and western boundaries of the refuge. Stop to
check the willows along the road in the spring and summer for
Yellow Warblers and Bell's Vireos. In the fall and early winter,
Long-eared and Short-eared Owls can be flushed from these
areas. But focus your major attention on the refuge pools and
the variety of waterbirds you will find at this extraordinary site.

TALL-GRASS PRAIRIE

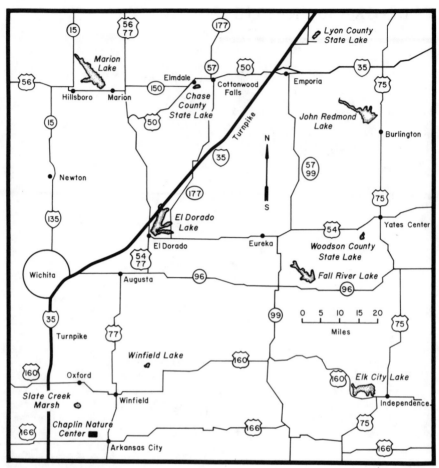

MAP 15. *Southern Tall-grass Prairie and Southwestern Forest-Prairie Mosaic*

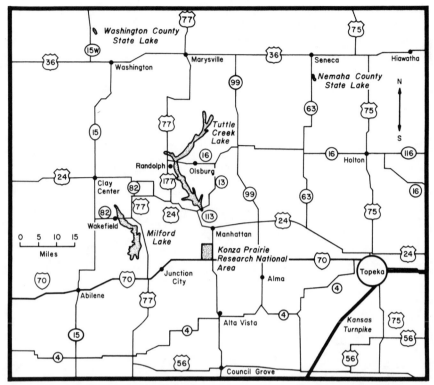

MAP 16. *Northern Tall-grass Prairie*

ARKANSAS CITY, KANSAS

The Wichita Audubon Society maintains the Chaplin Nature Center, an area of about 200 acres along the Arkansas River in Cowley County, composed of mature deciduous forest, small patches of prairie, old fields, and cultivated lands. The bird list totals more than 200 species, including a surprising variety of shorebirds attracted to the sandbars along the river during migration as well as Chuck-will's-widow, Pileated Woodpecker, Carolina Chickadee, Wood Thrush, Summer Tanager, Rose-breasted Grosbeak, and Indigo Bunting during the breeding season. The expected variety of passerines can be seen during migration, but in winter Bald Eagles frequent the river and mixed species flocks of sparrows, including large numbers of Harris' Sparrows, occur throughout the site. Expect Wild Turkey any time during the year.

Down from their summer home at the edge of the taiga, Harris' Sparrows fill fencerows and windbreaks across the entire breadth of the region.

Visitors are welcome seven days a week from sunrise to sunset, but please register at the orientation shelter. To reach the area, proceed west from Arkansas City on U.S. 166 for 3 miles from the junction with U.S. 77. At this point turn right (north) and continue 2.3 miles to the entrance road into the nature center on your right.

COTTONWOOD FALLS, KANSAS

Kansas Highway 177 threads its way through, around, and over the Flint Hills from north of Manhattan south to El Dorado. About midway along this route is Chase County State Fishing Lake, a small lake formed by the damming of Prather Creek in a delightful prairie setting. The lake attracts the expected variety of waterfowl during migration. Although there are some small stands of deciduous trees that increase the diversity of terrestrial bird species, the chance to walk in the tall-grass prairie makes this stop worthwhile.

When going either north or south on K177, turn west on Main Street in Cottonwood Falls, just south of the bridge over the Cottonwood River. Continue west for 2.6 miles and turn left at the gate to the state lake. At 0.4 mile from the entrance the parking lot on your left provides a good view of the lake. The road dead-ends in a loop 0.9 mile beyond in a small grove of elm, osage orange, willow, and cottonwood at the upper reach of the lake. Park at any of the several turn-offs and walk west to explore the prairie.

For some good roadside birding through well-managed tall-grass prairie, return to the entrance of the state lake and turn left (west again). You will reach the town of Elmdale in about 3 miles. Turn left on U.S. 50 for about 1 mile and then turn right (west) on K150. This highway goes straight west for 17 miles to intersect U.S. 77 just east of Marion. During the breeding season watch for Upland Sandpipers on the fence posts, and Grasshopper Sparrows, Eastern Meadowlarks, and Dickcissels in the fields. Common Nighthawks can be seen at almost any time of day, but if you are travelling this way soon after sunset, stop and listen for Common Poorwills near sites where the terraced benches of the hills expose limestone outcrops. If you are here during the period from a half hour before to an hour after dawn, listen for the "booming" of the Greater Prairie-chicken near the hilltops where the grass is shorter. In winter, expect to see Northern Harriers, Red-tailed Hawks, and Rough-legged Hawks with a chance for Horned Larks and Lapland Longspurs along the roadsides if the fields are snow-covered. The following are some suggested stops. In about 2.2 miles from U.S. 50 you can pull off at a pasture gate and corral and spend a little time look-ing and listening for prairie birds; this could be a good spot to hear Common Poorwills after dark. In another 1.7 miles the lane into a microwave tower should be a good place to listen for Greater Prairie-chickens. After another 1.3 miles pull off near a gas pipeline utility shed and walk the side road south for a short distance. A shelterbelt across which the road passes at 2.6 miles from this last side road provides the chance to see different spe-cies, especially in winter. After you cross the Marion County line about 9 miles from u.s. 50, the amount of tall-grass prairie along the roadside decreases markedly.

From the mixed-grass prairie with its post-rock fencelines to the forest-prairie mosaic of Missouri, the Upland Sandpiper binds earth and sky together in its nuptial display.

EL DORADO, KANSAS

For finding waterfowl during migration and in winter on El Dorado Lake in the southern Flint Hills, go east on U.S. 54 from the
junction with U.S. 77 in El Dorado for 5.3 miles, turn left (north)
on K177 for 4.2 miles, and then turn left into the Blue Stem Point
Area of El Dorado State Park (permit required). Follow any of
the park roads that take you close to the water's edge and scan
the lake for the expected grebes, geese, and ducks. Although
there are extensive areas of mowed grass and a high density of
developed campgrounds, patches of upland tall-grass prairie occur with the characteristic assemblage of Eastern Meadowlarks,
Grasshopper Sparrows, Dickcissels, and Upland Sandpipers
during the breeding season.

A greater variety of habitats can be explored by turning left on
K177 as you come out of the state park and proceed north for 3.4
miles. There is a small place to park, and you can walk into the
El Dorado Lake Wildlife Management Area south of Durechon
Creek where a cattail marsh and riparian forest border the creek.
More ample parking at the end of a short road 0.7 mile north on
K177, just over the bridge, will also provide access to the wildlife
area north of the creek's entry into the lake.

━━━━━━━━━━

To the east of this city there is excellent birding at the Flint Hills National Wildlife Refuge (see Burlington KS), located in the valley of the Neosho River. Another good site that will allow you to search upland habitats in this area is at the 700-acre Lyon County State Fishing Lake, northeast of Emporia. The lake attracts a wide variety of waterfowl and other waterbirds like grebes, cormorants, gulls, and terns during migration; the upland areas have become a prairie woodland because of the extensive invasion of cedar, elm, hackberry, and dogwood thickets, providing habitat for many passerine species during all seasons. There are several Greater Prairie-chicken booming grounds in the uplands surrounding the lake. It would be worthwhile to contact the Kansas Department of Wildlife and Parks in Emporia (P.O. Box 1525, Emporia KS 66801) for locations and the names of landowners from whom to seek permission to trespass.

To reach this area, leave I-35 in Emporia at exit 131, turn north on Burlingame Road and continue for 7.5 miles to the intersection with K99. Continue on K99 for 0.9 mile and then turn right (east) on K170. After 2 miles turn left (north) on a gravel road that will take you to the lake. As you approach the lake from the south from mid-October through late April, check *mowed* hayfields for Smith's Longspurs. This area is probably your best chance for seeing this species anywhere in the tall-grass prairie, except during the most severe winters. Also keep alert for Short-eared Owls at dusk and dawn over the prairies that border the road. At 1.1 miles from this corner, the road that angles off to your left will bring you to a bluff overlooking the upper end of the lake in an area partly mowed but with extensive patches of trees and shrubs. Long-eared Owls often roost in the dense stands of cedars along this side of the lake in the winter. During the breeding season, Bell's Vireos and Rufous-sided Towhees can be found nesting in the thickets.

To reach the dam, return to the north-south road, turn left (north), drive for about 0.5 mile, cross the dam, and park in the camping area on the north side of the lake just beyond the spillway. From this point walk into the game management area to the north and west where there is well-developed cover and a minimum of developmental disturbance.

JUNCTION CITY, KANSAS

In the winter when the upper end of Milford Lake (see Wakefield KS) becomes frozen, the best locations for waterfowl are in the dam area of this impoundment on the Republican River just upstream from its confluence with the Smoky Hill. This area also provides terrestrial habitats characteristic of riparian areas of the Flint Hills Uplands.

To reach the lake, go north from 1-70 at exit 295, just west of Junction City, on u.s. 77 for 4.5 miles, and then turn left (west) on k57. At 1.1 miles from this corner turn right on a road that comes to a parking area in about 0.5 mile, adjacent to the outflow channel from the reservoir. This is an excellent location for gulls and terns during migration and in the winter for arctic rarities like the Glaucous Gull. It is also a good place to explore the open riparian habitat on the west side of the channel during all seasons for the typical passerine species. Return to k57 and turn right. Stay on k57 as it proceeds toward the dam, but at 1 mile, just before crossing the dam, turn right at the sign indicating the Milford Fish Hatchery and proceed above the outflow channel to a crossroad in 0.5 mile. If you proceed straight across this intersection, the road will take you to the swimming beach area and access to a small lake for waterfowl viewing; however, this road is usually closed during the winter and early spring, but you can walk in if you like. To gain more convenient access to this lake, turn left on the hatchery road. In 0.7 mile follow this road to the right. Turn left at the first opportunity and follow a road that loops through a cottonwood grove adjacent to a small cattail marsh. There is a space to park just before the road returns to the hatchery road. This is a good place to do some looking around at any time of the year, but especially in winter since this marsh is fed by a large spring and thus is usually open. Wintering Common Yellowthroats have occurred here along with occasional Marsh Wrens, and you can regularly expect such winter birds as Swamp Sparrows. In early June, you can usually find Willow Flycatchers, and rails are present during spring and fall migration. The Milford Fish Hatchery is open to visitors from 8 a.m. to 5 p.m., Monday through Friday, and from 9 a.m. to 4 p.m. on Saturday and Sunday. Park in the visitors' parking area and ask at the hatchery for permission to walk down to the lake to look for waterfowl.

To reach the reservoir, return to K57, turn right, and then turn left in 0.1 mile. This road will take you to a number of vantage points along the lake. Another access to the lower part of the reservoir can be reached by turning west on K57 and following the signs to reach K244. At this intersection turn right (north) and continue for 2 miles to the entrance of the Rolling Hills Area. Follow this road and its various side roads to reach the lake. You should check a number of large pine plantings in this area in the winter; both Northern Saw-whet and Long-eared Owls have been found here. Although this gate is also closed in the winter, some of the pine plantings are within a mile of K244, and it is worth walking in.

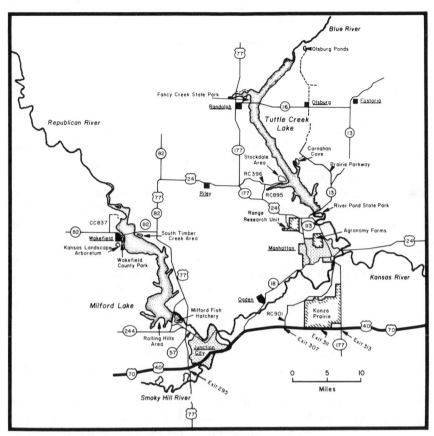

MAP 17. *Junction City–Manhattan Area*

To find the greatest variety of species at all seasons it is most productive to visit several sites around Tuttle Creek Lake. Proceed north out of Manhattan on u.s. 24 (Tuttle Creek Boulevard); 4.4 miles beyond the traffic light at the intersection of Tuttle Creek Boulevard and Bluemont Avenue turn right onto the entrance road to River Pond State Park. After making the turn, continue directly across to a drive that takes you along the Big Blue River below the outlet of the reservoir. From November to April, but especially from December through February, look for Bald Eagles in the large cottonwood trees on the east side of the river or just flying up and down the river below the outlet. In winter, Mallard, Gadwall, Common Goldeneye, and Common Merganser are abundant here, along with numerous gulls. Although Ring-billed are the most numerous, there are always a few Herring Gulls, and Glaucous Gulls have been present for a few weeks in recent winters. This short drive soon joins the entrance road. Turn right and continue as the road approaches the face of the dam and goes around the outlet. Stop the car in the parking lot at the top of a slight rise on the east side of the river and scan the waterfowl in the river, especially if the outflow is high. Wintering Common Loons and an occasional Old Squaw turn up here. In April and May, Bonaparte's Gulls, Forster's Terns, Black Terns, and sometimes a Caspian Tern can be seen among the more common species of gulls feeding in the river.

Leave this parking lot, turn right (east), and enter River Pond State Park (permit required). If you do not want to purchase a permit, you can leave your car at this parking lot and walk in because a permit is not required in the U.S. Corps of Engineers areas. The state park is the best all-around, all-seasons birding area in the vicinity. If you have time for just this stop, it will be worthwhile. As you drive into the park, take the first road to your right, just after the turn-off to the information shelter. Then turn right again to take the loop into the camping area located beside a series of beaver ponds fed by water seeping under the dam. Park near the most northerly pond and walk through the camping area along the east side of the ponds all the way to where this stream enters the Big Blue River. These ponds, excel-

The cacophony of the Greater Prairie-chicken lek rises above the April wind throughout the tall-grass prairie. Two males meet at the boundary between their territories, and the bird on the right begins a passive response evoked by his neighbor's stronger threat.

lent for water and marsh birds, are best as you might expect outside the summer camping season. But even then, Least Bitterns and Great-tailed Grackles have been found nesting in the cattails. If any Green-winged Teal, American Wigeon, or Northern Shoveler are overwintering, this is the place to find them. In migration the vegetation along the margins of these ponds, especially along the levee south of the washroom, is excellent. In addition to the abundant Yellow-rumped and Orange-crowned Warblers, Yellow, Black-and-white, Black-throated Green, Blackpoll, and Magnolia Warblers and American Redstart are fairly regular. From March into May the sequence of migrant sparrows can be observed starting with the wintering American Tree, Song, and Harris's Sparrows, followed by White-crowned, White-throated, Lincoln's, and Fox Sparrows, and finally Chipping and Clay-colored Sparrows. Both Eastern and Western Meadowlarks can be found in the fields adjacent to the campground throughout the year. Beginning in March, look for Wood Ducks swimming among the snags.

When you reach the end of the trail along the east side where it enters a parking lot, you can return to your car by going left (east) and looping back along the west side of the river ponds. In September and October and again in April and May, look for

Ospreys, which are regular here. The deeper water of these ponds attracts the expected variety of diving ducks as well as Eared, Horned, and Pied-billed Grebes and American White Pelicans. Keep a look out for the occasional Common Loon swimming quite apart from the hundreds of Double-crested Cormorants.

When you return to your car, go back to the road along the face of the dam where you first turned into the campground area, turn right (east), and follow the signs to the swimming beach, parking by the bathhouse. All but the rarest of waterfowl that migrate through Kansas have been seen here. In the spring, if the outflow from the reservoir is high enough to partly flood the field below the bathhouse and depending upon the week of migration, this is one of the few local places for shorebirds: not only the "peeps" and small plovers, but also Black-bellied Plovers, both yellowlegs, Pectoral Sandpipers, American Avocets, and a few Hudsonian Godwits can be seen.

Back in your car, return past the outlet to U.S. 24 and turn right. At 0.5 mile turn right again on K13, continuing over the dam. You cannot park on the dam, but there are parking areas at both the east and west ends where you can stop and look for rafts of waterfowl on the reservoir during migration and inspect the trees along the western side that mark the old river channel for eagles and Ospreys. Continue on K13. At 5.2 miles from its junction with U.S. 24, turn left off K13 onto the hard-surfaced Prairie Parkway. This road climbs up through tall-grass prairie once considered as a proposed site for the prairie national park. (Indeed, before this road was built, this is the area in which then-Secretary of the Interior Stuart Udall was met alighting from his helicopter by an irate shotgun-toting rancher.) Now, however, from April through July, watch for Upland Sandpipers on the fence posts and Western Kingbirds on the wires. Where fence-lines are wooded, expect Blue Grosbeaks and Loggerhead Shrikes.

At 4.8 miles from K13 a poorly marked, almost hidden turn-off on your left leads to Carnahan Cove; if you come to the bridge over Carnahan Creek at the bottom of the hill, you have gone too far. Turn in on this gravel road, continue for 0.8 mile, and turn right onto a hardtop road into the campground area. Continue to bear left as the road follows the valley of Carnahan Creek to a protected cove on the east side of Tuttle Creek Lake. This road will eventually loop back in about 2.5 miles to the point where you first entered the campground area. Depending upon season and water level, Carnahan Cove can provide quite a variety of ducks and geese, gulls and terns, grebes, American White Pelicans and Double-crested Cormorants, and herons, but there is little shorebird habitat. The uplands in the park area are largely tall-grass prairie, although there is some riparian forest in the valley. When you leave Carnahan Cove, you can turn right to return to Manhattan or turn left to reach the upper end of Tuttle Creek Lake. (See the tours described for Olsburg KS, a town about 6 miles north on the Prairie Parkway.)

To reach another site on the west side of Tuttle Creek Lake from the River Pond State Park area, instead of turning right on K13 towards Carnahan Cove, continue west on U.S. 24 to the Stockdale Area. Watch for the sign and then turn right (north) on Riley County 895. At 1.7 miles from U.S. 24 you will come to a "T"; if you turn left here and go west up the valley of Mill Creek, in about 1 mile you will come to a nesting colony of Great Blue Herons in the tall sycamores along the creek on your left. The herons arrive in mid-March and remain into the summer. This heronry is on private land so please do not trespass. You can see the activity in the colony quite well from the road. If you turn right at the "T," you will reach the Stockdale Recreation Area (a U.S. Army Corps of Engineers area) in 1.6 miles. Expect a variety of waterfowl here during migration, and Wild Turkeys occur on the south side of Mill Creek cove.

When you return to U.S. 24 on Riley Co. 895, turn left back towards Manhattan, but then turn right after 3.5 miles on a gravel road that winds through uplands of tall-grass prairie. During the breeding season you can expect Upland Sandpipers, Dickcissels, Eastern Meadowlarks, and Grasshopper Sparrows with Brown Thrashers, Field Sparrows, and Bell's Vireos in the thickets. In winter there will be flocks of American Tree Sparrows in the thickets and Northern Harriers cruising the prairies. At 1.9 miles from U.S. 24 on your left you will come to an entrance gate to the Range Research Unit of Kansas State University. Pull in here and stop, then look to your left (southwest). The ridge running south from the road is the location of a Greater Prairie-chicken lek that can be viewed from this spot if you arrive here about one-half hour before sunrise from mid-March until mid-May. Birds are present here all year long, but they are difficult to find when not displaying.

Continue on this gravel road. In 1.5 miles this road intersects Seth Childs Road (K113). Continue across to Marlatt Avenue, which meets U.S. 24 (Tuttle Creek Boulevard) in 2.2 miles, about

2.5 miles north of Bluemont Avenue where you started this tour. If you are driving Marlatt Avenue from late October to April, inspect the tops of the utility poles south of the road for the Prairie Falcons that feed on the flocks of sparrows and blackbirds frequenting the fields of the Agronomy Farm of Kansas State University.

Konza Prairie Research Natural Area, a Nature Conservancy site administered by the Division of Biology at Kansas State University, is about 13 square miles of largely undisturbed, virgin tall-grass prairie and associated riparian deciduous forest. As in all grasslands, bird diversity is not great, but Konza Prairie is probably the most reliable site in the region for finding Henslow's Sparrows from mid-April until August. There is also a blind available (reservations required) from mid-March to mid-May for viewing the display of the Greater Prairie-chicken. Other nesting species of note are Common Poorwill, Chuckwill's-widow, Sedge Wren (July to September only), Bell's Vireo, Louisiana Waterthrush, Kentucky Warbler, and Blue Grosbeak. During October, migrant flocks of Le Conte's Sparrows are easily found. Entry is by prior permission only; write Director, Konza Prairie Research Natural Area, Division of Biology, Kansas State University, Manhattan KS 66506.

To reach Konza Prairie, go south on K177 out of Manhattan. Just after crossing the Kansas River, turn right on McDowell Creek Road (Riley County 901) and continue for 6.4 miles. Turn left onto the entrance road and proceed for about a quarter mile to a graveled space on your left where you can park. When walking on Konza Prairie stay on the trails and fireguards; do not walk across the prairie since you might inadvertently disturb ongoing experiments. If you make prior arrangements, directions can be given for finding the birds you would most like to see. There is another entrance to Konza Prairie off I-70 (see I-70 Transect) that you might prefer if you are solely interested in upland prairie birds.

MARION, KANSAS

Formed by the damming of the North Cottonwood River, Marion Lake lies on the western side of the Flint Hills about midway between the northern and southern borders of Kansas. The terrestrial habitats in the vicinity of the lake are in agricultural production, but the Kansas Department of Wildlife and Parks has set aside a number of wildlife areas adjacent to the lake that provide considerable habitat along fencerows and wildlife plantings for characteristic edge species. The main attraction of this site, however, is the variety of waterbirds that use the lake during both migration and winter, as long as the water stays open.

To reach Marion Lake, travel west on u.s. 56 out of Marion for about 4 miles and turn right (north) at the sign indicating Marion Dam and Lake. Continue on this hardtop road to reach the dam in about 2 miles. For a better view of the lake, continue for 1 mile north and 1 mile west to reach Cottonwood Point Campground (no entry fee, but there is a charge for camping). Although there is minimum vegetation along the lake and the campground area is mowed, this is a good site for waterfowl viewing.

For greater variety of both terrestrial and aquatic habitats, drive west out of Marion on u.s. 56 for 8 miles, turn right (north) on a hard-surfaced road, and continue for 6.1 miles to the entrance to the Durham Cove Recreational Area. This site provides primitive camping (no fee) and access to the upper end of Marion Lake and associated riparian habitat. Just 0.7 mile beyond the entrance to the Durham Cove site, the north-south road turns and crosses the North Cottonwood River. As the road turns, the road to the left leads to a parking area. Turn off and park here, and then walk across the bridge to view a well-developed cattail marsh with nesting Yellow-headed Blackbirds, as well as other marsh species, to the right of the bridge and to the left, cottonwood-willow sloughs. This is an excellent puddle duck and wader area and, if mudflats are exposed, a good site for shorebirds as well. All of these are most easily observed from either end of the bridge where there is space to stand out of traffic. There is another road into this section of the Marion Wildlife Management Area about 0.5 mile on your left beyond the bridge.

At the north end of the bridge, there is a gravel road to the right (east). If you follow this road for 3 miles you intersect a hard-surfaced road. At this point turn right (south) and continue for 3 more miles. The road you are on bends to the left here, but turn right and then immediately to the left onto a marginal gravel road to reach another section of the Marion Wildlife Management Area about midway down the east side of the lake. If this road is not passable because of wet weather, park the car and walk in; it is only about 0.5 mile to the boundary of the wildlife area. To return to the dam, continue 2 miles east from the turn-off into the wildlife area; then turn right (south) and continue for about another 3 miles.

OLSBURG, KANSAS

This small farm community is the starting point for a tour of the
upper end of Tuttle Creek Lake. The best time to make this visit
is during spring waterfowl and shorebird migration periods or
in fall and early winter during periods when the hunting season
is not open. From town go east on K16 and turn left (north) at
the first opportunity (approximately 0.4 mile east of the street
through the Olsburg business district). After 2.5 miles you will
come to a "Y"; bear left and continue. At 5.6 miles from K16 an
old school house is on your left, and the road makes a "T." Turn
right and then left at the first chance (about 0.1 mile farther); go
for 0.9 mile from this corner and make another turn to the left
into one area of the Tuttle Creek Wildlife Management Area.
This lane is usually passable in all but the wettest weather and
leads to a parking lot on your right in 0.4 mile. Pull in here, park,
and walk north toward the trees that border the Olsburg Ponds;
if they contain water, the ponds are excellent for geese, both dab-
bling and diving ducks, gulls and terns, shorebirds, rails and
herons. Water level is critical: no water or too much water elimi-
nates the habitat. A second parking lot 0.7 mile farther down the
lane is adjacent to a deeper pond. If the first site is dry, try the
second pond. If the first pond is shallow enough to be excellent
for shorebirds, the waterfowl may be in the second pond. Also,
do not overlook the cultivated fields and the narrow stands of
riparian forest in this area.

Return to K16, turn right (west), drive through Olsburg, crossing Tuttle Creek Lake on the Randolph Bridge (the longest
bridge in Kansas), and turn right on Riley Co. 893 about 7 miles
from Olsburg towards Fancy Creek State Park (permit required).
This road will end in 1.3 miles at a large parking lot associated
with an abandoned marina no longer usable as a result of silting
in the upper reaches of the reservoir. From November to April
this is a good spot to see Bald Eagles flying over the water,
perched on the dead trees that follow the old river channel, or in
the trees on the island just across from you (the remains of the
old townsite of Randolph). During migration the expected waterfowl can be seen here as well, and the now shallow basin of
the marina itself provides shorebird habitat. You may also note

concentrations of waterfowl and shorebirds on the north side of the Fancy Creek cove, but they are too far away to identify from this side. As you return to K16, stop at the parking space on your left at the park entrance sign and spend some time looking along the wooded creek margin to the east of the road for a variety of passerines in all seasons, including nesting Louisiana Water-thrushes.

To get to the north side of the cove, at K16 turn right (west) and continue about 0.5 mile to the stop sign at U.S. 77. Turn right (north) and continue for 2.2 miles, stopping at the north end of the bridge over Fancy Creek. To the east, except in the driest of years, check the shallow lake for waterfowl and shorebirds in the spring and fall. In late summer and early fall this is a good place to see post-breeding egrets and other herons. You can get closer to this lake if you drive 0.6 mile beyond where you are stopped and turn right onto a gravel road (eventually this becomes a mud road that should not be traveled in wet weather). But you can park along this road and walk down to the northeast corner of this lake where some trees provide cover for viewing. You can also walk east from here through fields to reach other, smaller ponds, but the amount of water they contain depends upon recent lake levels. In September and October Marsh Wrens are almost a certainty in the weedy vegetation along with lingering Common Yellowthroats and migrant Savannah and LeConte's Sparrows. Eventually a creek will block your way, but if you walk north until you intersect the road, you can then walk farther toward the reservoir to investigate the birds you saw from the marina at Fancy Creek State Park. You can also go back to your car and drive this road if it is dry. During shorebird migration it is worth checking the flats at the end of this road, since this site is the best location in the area for waders. Then return to U.S. 77 and turn left (south) to reach K16 in 1.6 miles. At this point you can return to Olsburg, or, if you continue for about 12 miles south on U.S. 77, you can turn left on Riley Co. 396 to reach the Stockdale Recreation Area (see Manhattan KS).

OXFORD, KANSAS

Slate Creek Marsh, a small area of shallow pools with bordering marsh vegetation and mudflats, attracts a variety of shorebirds, rails, herons, and waterfowl if rainfall has been sufficient to maintain the water level in the habitat. Thus, it is usually a good spot in spring, but poor in late summer and fall. The area is on private land, but an unmaintained township road bisects the site, providing fair access for viewing.

From the blinker light on U.S. 160 in Oxford, turn south on a hardtop road and continue for 8 miles. Then turn right (west) on a dirt road and proceed with caution. In wet weather this road may be impassable immediately at the turn-off, and even in dry weather it eventually becomes impassable. Park and continue west on foot. Look for Carolina Chickadees in the elm and osage orange fencerows along the edge of the road. In about 0.5 mile the road drops into the marshy lowlands.

WAKEFIELD, KANSAS

From this town on the eastern edge of Clay County at the upper end of Milford Lake you can reach a variety of habitats which provide good birding during every season. Of course, spring and fall are the best for the greatest diversity of bird species because of the attractiveness of the open water and littoral habitats to migratory species. But even during winter when the lake is frozen at its upper end, the terrestrial habitats are diverse enough to offer both the normal variety of winter birds and the hope for wandering northern finches and stragglers from the western mountains.

Two sites adjacent to the town of Wakefield are worth investigating. Just west of the bridge over Milford Lake on the east end of Wakefield, turn south from K82 on Birch Street to reach Wakefield County Park. Although there are no terrestrial habitats worth noting here, this park does provide good access to the lake for waterfowl viewing. Two blocks farther west on K82, turn south on Dogwood Street, continue straight through the park onto a gravel road at 0.4 mile from K82, turn right 0.1 mile farther, and bear left after 0.2 mile to reach the main gate of the Kansas Landscape Arboretum (open all year from 8 a.m. to dusk). This 193-acre area provides a mix of natural areas and plantings of over 400 varieties of trees and shrubs. Since many of these horticultural varieties (hawthornes and flowering crabs) are attractive to frugivorous birds, an hour or two of your time can be quite fruitful, especially in winter. Just park in one of the spaces provided, and walk the roads and trails through the area.

The best shorebird and wader habitat on Milford Lake, located on a game refuge maintained by the Kansas Department of Wildlife and Parks, can be reached by going west out of Wakefield on K82 and turning right (north) on Clay Co. 837. Continue north for 2 miles, and then turn right (east) on a gravel road just where the hardtop bends to the left. At 1.2 miles from this corner turn on a road to your left and park. Walk east toward the lake through the cultivated fields to several shallow ponds and inlets at the point where the Republican River enters the lake. Although worth visiting in the spring, this site is especially good in late summer and fall when it attracts herons and egrets, gulls and terns, and a variety of shorebirds. Among the more unusual species seen here have been Least Tern, Snowy Plover, and Long-billed Curlew.

When you return to your car, drive this gravel road north through cultivated fields, old fields, and hedgerows and along a hillside forest of oak, elm, hackberry, and a few hickories, stopping from time to time to explore these habitats. This road ends in 1 mile at the Republican River in an area of dead trees, which provide convenient snags for wintering raptors like Bald Eagles.

To reach upland forest habitat, go east out of Wakefield on K82 over the causeway across Milford Lake and turn right into the South Timber Creek Recreational Area, maintained by the U.S. Army Corps of Engineers. Turn right immediately on Interior Road No. 2, bear left at the first road junction, and reach a parking lot at the end of the road, 0.3 mile from the corner, next to shelter #2. Walk the interpretive trail that starts adjacent to this parking area through an upland forest of elm, oak, hickory, honey locust, and cedar. Although bird diversity is not especially great here, you will discover species not found in the other habitats; and if the cedar berry crop is good, you should especially be alert for wintering Townsend's Solitaires.

128

Tall-grass Prairie

Devils Creek in the watershed of the Little Blue River drains an area of intense, diversified agriculture near the Nebraska border. Washington County State Fishing Lake has been developed in this valley and provides a small island (about 500 acres) of more natural habitat attractive to a variety of birds throughout the year. Although there are no riparian forest stands, copses of cottonwood, elm, and honey locust and an edge of willows along the lake offer some terrestrial habitat diversity and provide opportunities for observing migrant passerines. The breeding birds are those expected in this part of the region—Dickcissels and Field Sparrows in the brushy upland prairie, and Northern Orioles and Warbling Vireos along the margins of the lake.

To reach this site travel approximately 6.5 miles west of Washington on U.S. 36 and turn north onto K15W. Continue north for 5.1 miles, turn right (east) for 3 miles, turn left (north) for another 3 miles, and finally turn left (west) to reach the park entrance in 0.6 mile. To view the lower end of the lake for waterfowl, turn left at the first opportunity. For a greater variety of habitats, turn right instead of left and proceed for 0.4 mile; then turn left, following this short road to its end, and park. This shallow upper end of the lake is good for shorebirds in migration and from spring through fall for waterfowl and herons, but diversity is greatest during migration. Marsh Wrens and Swamp Sparrows, occuring during migration, are most noticeable in October.

WICHITA, KANSAS

In the valley of the Arkansas River at its union with the Little
Arkansas River, this urban center is at the juncture of the southern tall-grass prairie to the east and the sand prairies to the west.
Thus, the city can be a base for your exploration of a number of
bird-finding places in southcentral Kansas. Additionally three
sites within the city are worth the short amount of time it takes
to survey them for birds, especially at the heights of passerine
migration in the spring and fall.

Oak Park is a small area northwest of the city center. To reach
this site exit I-135 at 13th Street (exit 8) and proceed west on 13th
Street for 1.2 miles. Then turn left on Waco and continue south
to 11th Street in 0.3 mile. Turn right on 11th and go 0.8 mile to
the entrance to Oak Park. Turn right into the park and follow the
road along the bank of the Little Arkansas River. About 0.2 mile
from the park entrance, you cross a stone bridge. Turn right
here, park, and then explore the trail along the top of an em-
bankment through a surprisingly wild riparian forest of hackberry, mulberry, walnut, and honey locust with an understory of
cedar, redbud, and wahoo. In summer you can expect to see
Red-bellied Woodpecker, White-breasted Nuthatch, Blue-gray
Gnatcatcher, Northern Oriole, Rose-breasted Grosbeak, and
other species characteristic of riparian habitats. In winter there
are mixed species flocks of sparrows, including White-throated
and Lincoln Sparrows. This trail eventually comes out into a
more developed section of the park, but there are a number of
side trails off to your left that will allow you to loop back to
where you parked after covering about three-eighths of a mile.

If you continue west from Oak Park on 11th Street for about
0.5 mile, you enter Sim Park. Evergreen plantings along this
drive are worth checking in the winter for Yellow-bellied Sapsuckers, kinglets, and northern finches. Beyond the golf course,
the road turns south with the Arkansas River on your right and
riparian thickets on your left. At 0.7 mile from the park entrance
there is a side road into a picnic area where you can park and
spend some time on foot. While Sim Park has more open vegetation with smaller thickets and less understory, many of the
more typical riparian birds can be found here. During the sum-

mer you should keep alert for Mississippi Kites that are urban nesters in this area.

If you would like to briefly get away from the urban environment, visit Pawnee Prairie Park on the west side of the city. This mix of habitats—an undeveloped site of old fields and riparian thickets of elm, hackberry, cottonwood, and walnut along Cowskin Creek—attracts a variety of birds. It is particularly worthwhile during passerine migration and in the winter. To reach Pawnee Prairie Park, go west on Kellogg Avenue (u.s. 54) past Tyler Road and turn left (south) on a gravel road marked by the B-47 perched on a pedestal at Air Capitol Memorial Park. This turn-off is 8 miles west of the Kellogg Avenue exit on I-135 and 3 miles west of the exit from I-235. Go south for just 0.1 mile and turn right on Harry Street, which might be muddy, reaching a parking lot in 0.1 mile. Park here and walk the nature trail through the park.

Tall-grass
Prairie

WINFIELD, KANSAS

The Winfield City Lake annually turns up uncommon species of
waterfowl like scoters, Oldsquaws, and Common Loons. This is
especially true during the winter months when it sometimes remains completely ice-free due to its southerly location in the
state.

Take U.S. 77 north out of Winfield; at 8.5 miles north of the
intersection of U.S. 77 and U.S. 160 in Winfield, turn right (east)
on a hardtop road that continues to the north end of the dam at
6.5 miles from the turn-off. The road makes a "T" here. You can
go right and enter the south shore recreational area on the other
side of the dam with access to the lake for waterfowl viewing.
But for better terrestrial habitats, with less opportunity for scan-
ning the open waters of the lake, turn left at the "T," go 0.9 mile,
and then turn right to reach the north shore recreational area.
Drive to the very end of this road, approximately 1.5 miles from
the turn-off, to the tent camping and picnic area. Some stands of
elm, walnut, and honey locust along the shore as well as some
small marshy areas in the shallow coves are good for migrant
passerines.

To reach the east end where Timber Creek flows into the lake,
as you come out of the north shore recreation area turn right and
go about 0.5 mile to the first road on your right. Go east on this
road for 2 miles, then turn right (south), drive to the end of the
road, and park. There is good riparian forest adjacent to the lake
here and some development of cattail marshes.

From Winfield you can reach a more mature riparian forest of
sycamore, cottonwood, elm, walnut, and hackberry along the
Arkansas River by going west on U.S. 160 from its junction with
U.S. 77 for 6.5 miles. At this point bear left and continue for 0.2
mile to a stop sign near a cemetery. Turn left (south) here on
Cowley Co. 3 and drive for 4 miles, where you come to another
stop sign. Continue across this intersection onto a sand road for
about 0.5 mile and then park. You will note that the private property adjacent to this lane is posted, but you can find many species along the road and most of the land on the left side is open
for entry. Many of the species found at the Chaplin Nature Center (see Arkansas City KS) can be seen in the bottomlands here.

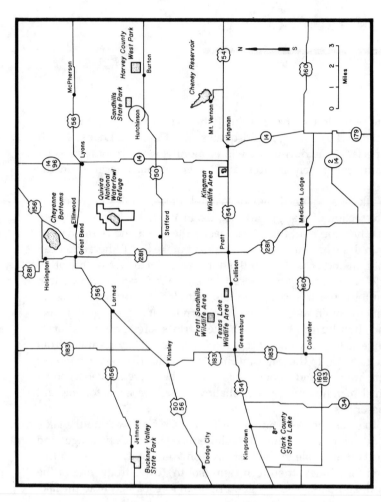

MAP 18. Southern Mixed-grass Prairie and Sand Prairie

SAND PRAIRIE

BURRTON, KANSAS

A mature riparian forest of cottonwood, hackberry, elm, and walnut along the Little Arkansas River is within the approximately 400 acres of Harvey County West Park. Although much of the area is mowed, park-like, and heavily used by campers on weekends, this site still provides a good list of species at all seasons since there are patches of brushy thickets, less disturbed forest areas, and two small ponds. Of particular note are nesting Wood Duck, Mississippi Kite, American Woodcock, Scissor-tailed Flycatcher, Orchard Oriole, and Rose-breasted Grosbeak. A good variety of vireos, warblers, thrushes, and sparrows can be seen during migration. In addition to more regular winter residents like Harris', White-crowned, and Song Sparrows, Red-breasted Nuthatches and Winter Wrens can also be found in appropriate habitats.

To reach the park, take u.s. 50 east out of Burrton KS. Four miles beyond the intersection of u.s. 50 with Harvey Co. 785 on the east side of Burrton, turn left (north) on Harvey Co. 793 and continue north for 3 miles. Then turn right (east) on Harvey Co. 566, reaching the entrance to the park on your left in 0.8 mile. The entrance road proceeds northward through the park, but you can take various turn-offs to reach a parking space so you can explore on foot some of the thickets of more natural vegetation west of the entrance as well as the borders of the small lakes. Then follow the main road all the way to the north entrance into the park, turn right (east), cross over the Little Arkansas River, and turn right onto a road that goes south along the east side of the river to a dead end in less than a mile. This side of the river is less disturbed, and there are fewer mowed areas; the birding is generally better than in the more developed parts of the park.

━━━━━━━━━━━━━━━━━

_____

*Sand
Prairie*

Small lakes and marshy sloughs, characteristic of the sand prairie, tend to be lost as land is used for agricultural production. One preserved site is the Texas Lake Wildlife Management Area, a small area of only 560 acres that provides suitable habitat for both migrant and nesting waterfowl, shorebirds, and marsh-dwelling species. To reach this site, go west on U.S. 54 approximately 4 miles from the center of Cullison, turn right (north) on a sand road, and proceed 2.5 miles to a parking area on your right. From here you can explore on foot through sand prairie habitat and along the marshy borders of several ponds and shallow lakes.

If you go 1 more mile west on U.S. 54 (approximately 5 miles from the center of Cullison) and turn right (north) on a sand road, you will reach the Pratt Sandhills Wildlife Management Area in 7 miles. The area extends on the west side of the road for 3 miles, and it begins 1 mile farther on the east side of the road and continues for 2 more miles. This road should be used with caution: it can be slick in wet weather; the sand may be too deep in dry weather for automobiles, especially compacts; furthermore, there are no established parking areas. A number of shelterbelts planted on the area have increased the avian species diversity. Expect Black-billed Magpies, and with a little luck you may discover Lesser Prairie-chickens on this site, about as far north and east as they range in Kansas.

Three miles beyond the northern boundary of the wildlife area you come to a hardtop road at a crossroads known as Hopewell. If you turn right (east) and continue for 7 miles and then turn right (south), you will come to U.S. 54 in 11.5 miles, 2 miles east of the center of Cullison.

GREAT BEND, KANSAS

The International Shorebird Survey conducted by the Manomet
Bird Observatory in Plymouth MA has clearly demonstrated the
importance of the Cheyenne Bottoms Wildlife Management Area
to the continent-wide populations of many shorebird species. Of
all birds counted at 210 sites across North America east of the
105th meridian during spring migration, more than 90 percent of
the White-rumped Sandpipers, Baird's Sandpipers, Stilt Sandpipers, Long-billed Dowitchers, and Wilson's Phalaropes were at
Cheyenne Bottoms. Furthermore, 59 percent of the Hudsonian
Godwits and 73 percent of the Marbled Godwits counted during
this period were at "The Bottoms." During the peak of the spring
shorebird migration, mid-April to mid-May, both species diversity and numbers are impressive, and Cheyenne Bottoms is the
place to be.

The Manomet report also indicates that during the fall migration shorebirds are less concentrated; yet 60 percent were still
accounted for by just ten sites. The situation is compounded in
the fall at Cheyenne Bottoms by the decreasing availability of
water during the summer and fall months. Maintenance water
for Cheyenne Bottoms was originally designed to be obtained
from the Arkansas River, but agricultural uses have so depleted
the water table during the growing season that the river disappears. In dry years small pools of water do remain, still providing satisfactory birding since the birds concentrate around these
patches of suitable habitat.

Although large numbers of individual birds characterize the
spring and all migratory periods, diversity during the summer
months remains high if there is sufficient water. Many shorebird
species stay rather than migrating north to their nesting areas,
and Cheyenne Bottoms itself maintains nesting populations of
grebes and cormorants, herons, egrets, bitterns, White-faced
Ibis, over a dozen species of waterfowl, rails, Wilson's Phalarope
and American Avocet, Forster's and Black Terns, and occasionally Least Terns. Furthermore, many reclusive marsh birds like
King Rail and Least Bittern are more frequently observed when
they are actively tending young.

To reach Cheyenne Bottoms, depart Great Bend north on

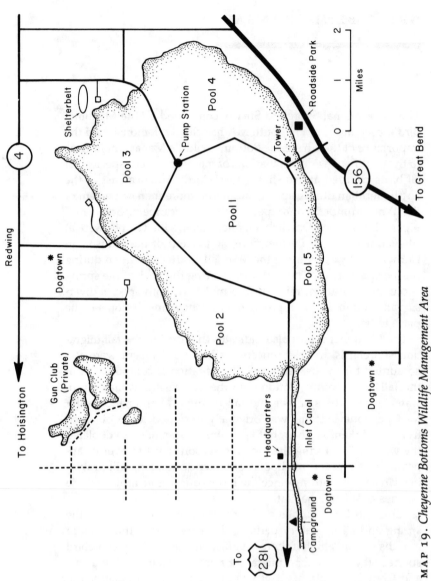

MAP 19. *Cheyenne Bottoms Wildlife Management Area*

The Yellow-headed Blackbird defends cattail castles with its version of the "spread" display and a raucous song.

U.S. 281 from its intersection with U.S. 56. At 6 miles turn right (east) onto a gravel road (approximately 4.5 miles south of Hoisington on U.S. 281). Within a mile you will drop into the natural depression that forms the basin in which this saline marsh had developed before man ever intruded. At 1.2 miles turn right into an undeveloped campground. Immediately to your right (west) a shelterbelt provides habitat for a variety of passerines, no matter what the season. In recent years there has been a Common Barn-owl around the campground, and Great Horned Owls and Eastern Screech-owls can be found as well. Bell's Vireo, Orchard Oriole, Western Kingbird, and Brown Thrasher regularly nest in the vicinity of the campground. During migration six to eight species of sparrows can regularly be found here, and there is always the chance for a vagrant Black-throated Gray or Townsend's Warbler. The inlet canal which flows along the south side of the campground is probably the most regular spot for seeing Green-backed Heron.

From the west entrance of the campground continue east for 0.8 mile to the first crossroad. To your left across this road you can obtain a checklist of birds at the headquarters building; there are also restrooms in the back (the only ones on the site). You can reach two prairie dog towns with Burrowing Owls from this point. To do this, turn right, cross the bridge over the inlet canal where several species of swallows congregate, and stop at the corral on your right, about 0.5 mile from the corner. The dog town is in the field to your right. If the owls are present, you will see them perched on the prairie dog burrows or flying low over the field. Occasionally they will be perched on the fence posts along the road. The field across the road to your left should be inspected for both waterfowl and shorebirds in the spring and summer as well as for Northern Harriers and Short-eared Owls. To reach the other dog town, continue for another 0.5 mile, turn left (east) for 2 miles, at which point the road turns south, continue for about 0.5 mile, and stop. The dog town is in the field to your right.

Return to refuge headquarters and continue east into "The Bottoms." The inlet canal to your right is good for grebes and ducks, while the marsh to your left is a good location for Cinnamon Teal, Sora, Virginia Rail, and King Rail. Three miles east of headquarters you reach the central pool (pool 1). If you are here during the spring shorebird migration, you should begin your search for concentrations of birds on the upwind sides of the pools, since the wind piles the water up on the downwind side, exposing mudflats and shallows to the windward. Although it is difficult to predict where the best birding will be, pools 3, 4, and 5 have consistently been the best. Jog a little to your right at this point and continue east along the north side of pool 5, stopping from time to time to check for birds on both sides of the road. After 2.5 miles you come to another intersection, bear to your right and then turn right on a road that will take you to K156 in 0.7 mile. At this point, turn left (northeast) and then turn in at the roadside park to your left. Stop here and scan the backside of pool 4. Depending on the water level, there is usually a variety of waterfowl and herons, including White-faced Ibis, using the sedge flats and shallow pools here and farther northeast along K156. This is a busy highway with few turn-offs to allow you to scan the fields, but, if you're careful as you pull off and reenter traffic, it is worthwhile to work your way up the highway for about 2 miles.

Return now to the entrance into Cheyenne Bottoms, just beyond the rest area, and then turn right at the tower to drive along the west side of pool 4. Occasionally stop, even if no concentrations of birds are in sight, and just scan the marsh to catch the occasional Least Bittern that might be up and flying. During spring and fall shorebird migration, stop and check any large flock of flying shorebirds for the Peregrine Falcon that has probably "spooked" them. In 2.3 miles you will come to a pump station on your right and a road off to the right between pools 3 and 4. This is another good location for concentrations of swallows. Turn right here and continue on the road between the pools. Pool 3 on your left, always a good place for a variety of herons, often has nesting Marsh Wrens. In 2 miles you will come to a road to your right. Continue past this road for 0.4 mile and turn off on a trail to your left that leads to a parking area for access to the backside of pool 3. Be sure the area is passable by your car; otherwise, walk in because the birding here is often good. You will notice a shelterbelt to the north. Explore this at any season, not only for passerines but also for owls.

Return to the road between pools 3 and 4 and drive back to the central pool (pool 1). At the pump station turn right. After 1.1 miles you will come to a road on your left which runs between pools 1 and 2 and intersects with the road that goes west toward refuge headquarters. Bear right at this corner to take the road between pools 3 and 2. Both sides of the road are often excellent for shorebirds and waterfowl. In about 1 mile a dirt road off to your right leads to a parking area that provides another way to the backside of pool 3, but this is impassable by car in wet weather. Continue north on the gravel road. You leave Cheyenne Bottoms at this point, but you don't leave the birds. Search the fields on both sides of the road, watching especially for Cattle Egrets in spring and summer and Long-billed Curlews during migration. Probably Buff-breasted Sandpipers are out there as well in early May, but it will take some diligent hunting to find them. About 1 mile from the road to the backside of pool 3 another prairie dog town on your left sometimes has Burrowing Owls. In 0.5 mile from this point the gravel road intersects highway K4 at the community of Redwing. Hoisington KS is about 6 miles west on K4, and the intersection with K156 is 8.5 miles east of this point.

If the weather has been dry and the dirt roads are passable, it would be worthwhile in any season to turn left (west) on K4, proceed 1 mile, then turn left (south), and continue for 2 miles at which point the road turns right (west). At this corner to your left a road into a parking area provides a way to the backside of pool 2. From here on the road is dirt, but if it is passable it is worth proceeding for 2 more miles until you see a shallow lake off to your right. This is private land, but you can bird well from the road. This area is sometimes quite good, providing a variety of shorebirds, relatively high concentrations of Soras, and a good chance for a Yellow-crowned Night-heron. In low rainfall years, however, it is frequently dry.

Continue on this road until it intersects a crossroad. Turn left (south) and continue 2 miles, crossing two low water bridges and then coming to a crossroad. Turn left (west) and continue for 1 mile, or as far as you can go. Again depending upon the water situation, shorebirding along this road is often quite good. Return back to the crossroad and turn left (south). In 1 mile you come to another crossroad; if you follow it to your left, it will also take you to the backside of pool 2. You will reach refuge headquarters 1 mile south from this intersection.

Although diversity is lower in the winter, Cheyenne Bottoms is still worth a visit. As long as there is open water there will be waterfowl, gulls, and perhaps some lingering shorebirds. Bald Eagles are common. Expect Rough-legged Hawks and Golden Eagles, and there is a good chance of seeing a Ferruginous Hawk. Lapland Longspurs are abundant, and careful scrutiny will reveal Chestnut-collared Longspurs as well.

GREENSBURG, KANSAS

The residents of this town in the middle of Kiowa County seem to have a comfortable relationship with the large number of Mississippi Kites that nest in their midst along the shaded streets. Stop and look for these delightful raptors from mid-spring until the end of September. It is also worthwhile during periods of waterfowl migration and in open winters to take North Bay Street in Greensburg north from u.s. 54 for just 0.5 mile to visit Kiowa County State Fishing Lake. Although small and primarily maintained for boating and fishing, the lake does provide migrating ducks and geese with a feeding and resting area. A gravel road very nearly encircles the lake, allowing easy observation of birds on the water. Also be sure to check the weedy patches and fields on the small north extension of the lake for feeding flocks of sparrows in the fall and winter; expect good numbers of White-crowned and Harris' Sparrows.

Mississippi Kites float over islands of cottonwoods, elms, and locusts formed by townsites and windbreaks in the sea of grass.

_____

If you just have a short period of time to spend birding during passerine migration, a good place to visit is the Dillon Outdoor Education Center. This small area has a bird list of more than 150 species, and even 16 species of waterfowl have been attracted to two small ponds. There is some natural cover of sand prairie and native trees, but horticultural varieties of trees and shrubs have been planted as well, including conifers that attract Red-breasted Nuthatches and Pine Siskins in the winter.

To reach the center, take K61 north out of Hutchinson. At 1.3 miles north of the intersection of 17th Street and K61, turn right (east) on 30th Street, and then turn left in 0.1 mile at the entrance road.

If you continue on K61 for 2.3 miles beyond the 30th Street intersection and turn right (east) on 56th Street, you reach the south parking lot of Sand Hills State Park on your left in 0.3 mile. This 1,123-acre park is an excellent example of undisturbed sand prairie with many ponds, sedge swales, and brushy vegetation on stabilized sand dunes. In the summer, Bell's Vireos, Black-billed Cuckoos, Yellow-breasted Chats, and Common Yellow-throats frequent the sandhills habitat, while in the cottonwood groves you will see Eastern Bluebirds, Blue Grosbeaks, and Blue-gray Gnatcatchers. During passerine migration, expect a variety of sparrows and warblers. Of special note are the small flocks of Le Conte's Sparrows that occur from mid- to late October.

Plans are to leave this park as undeveloped as possible, with access to the area only by way of hiking trails from the south and north parking lots. To reach the north parking lot, return to K61, turn right, and go north for 1 mile to 69th Street. Turn right here and continue to the parking lot on your right, 0.7 mile from the corner.

KINGMAN, KANSAS

Located in southcentral Kansas, the Byron Walker (Kingman) Wildlife Management Area and State Fishing Lake provides 4,462 acres along the South Fork of the Ninnescah River worth visiting at all seasons. The lake is less than 150 acres in size, but it attracts waterfowl during migration. A well-developed marsh on the west end of the lake provides nesting habitat for both ducks and marsh birds and feeding habitat for waders. An excellent riparian forest north and west of the lake—as well as at several other sites throughout the area with cottonwood, black walnut, elm, catalpa, and honey locust and a well-developed understory—attracts breeding species more typical of eastern Kansas, like the Wood Thrush. Good sand prairie covers much of the area, characteristically with swales, marshes, and small ponds in the watersheds draining into the Ninnescah River. Additionally, extensive wildlife plantings attract edge species like Bell's Vireo in the breeding season and mixed species flocks of sparrows in the winter. A visitor in any season can expect to find Wild Turkeys. Since most land in the vicinity is under intensive agriculture, this site, which extends for 4.5 miles on either side of u.s. 54, is a premier location for a variety of resident and migratory bird species.

To reach the Byron Walker Wildlife Management Area, proceed west on u.s. 54 for 7.9 miles from the junction with k14 in Kingman to the entrance into the Kingman State Fishing Lake on your right (north) at the east end of the wildlife area. You can reach the headquarters by continuing for another 1.3 miles and turning left (south). Maps are available here; these maps are quite useful, indicating the various habitats, access roads, and parking areas in the wildlife area.

For a brief tour of the site, turn in at the entrance to the state fishing lake (about 8 miles from the center of Kingman) and drive the loop through the camping area that borders the lake. When you return to the main road, turn right toward the entrance, and then turn right again on a sand road that borders the south side of the lake. After almost 1 mile you will be near the southwest corner of the lake; stop the car and climb up the dike to scan the marsh. Just beyond this point, the road comes close to the Ninnescah River, where you should also stop to search for birds. This road continues through stands of riparian forest interspersed with open spaces, which you should also stop to explore, and eventually intersects with a gravel road that runs along the northern boundary of the wildlife area. Turn left for about 0.2 mile and then turn left (south) again. On your right (west) is sand prairie habitat with numerous wildlife plantings, and on your left (east) riparian vegetation borders the road. After 0.5 mile the road angles to the right and soon intersects with U.S. 54 about 1 mile west of the road to headquarters. Turn right on U.S. 54 and continue west, stopping at several of the many turn-outs and parking areas in the next 2.5 miles that provide access through the fence to sand prairie and a few stands of riparian forest vegetation.

MT. VERNON, KANSAS

A number of roads on both the east and west sides of Cheney Reservoir allow you to reach the lakeshore for waterfowl viewing and provide access to the Cheney Wildlife Management Area. The best time to visit is during spring and fall migration, but the lake remains attractive to waterbirds during winter when a large wintering population of Bald Eagles around the reservoir from November through March provides an added incentive to visit. The terrestrial habitats have been enhanced by a variety of plantings, including fencerows of multiflora rose and shelterbelts of Russian olive, cedar, elm, and osage orange interspersed with patches of sand prairie.

To reach the west side of the lake, exit north from U.S. 54 on Kingman County Road 428 to Mt. Vernon. After 3 miles, turn right (east) and then turn left after 0.5 mile into Cheney State Park (permit required). Because of mowing and campground development, the state park provides little diversity in terrestrial habitats, but park roads do allow you to search the lake for water birds. Leave the park at the north exit and follow a hardtop road west, then north for a mile, then west again for another mile, and then north again; turn right (east) off this road, 4 miles after leaving the park, onto a gravel road that enters the southern end of the Cheney Wildlife Management Area where you can explore the lakeshore on foot.

Return to the paved road and continue west for 1 mile, then north for another mile, where you should then turn right (east) and continue past a developed area on the south side of the road until the road dead-ends in another section of the wildlife area. After checking out this area on foot, return to the west and turn right (north) on the first road. Take this gravel road north for 1 mile; then turn right (east) onto a hardtop road that ends in 0.5 mile in another section of the wildlife area with a particularly good stand of riparian forest. Because of the greater habitat diversity here, it should provide good birding during the periods of warbler migration.

When you leave this site, continue west on the paved road for 2 miles beyond the intersection with the gravel road and turn right (north) on K17. Drive north for 2 miles, then turn right (east) and continue for 1.3 miles, turning right off the paved road into another section of the wildlife area. This road ends at the North Fork of the Ninnescah River where you should search the exposed sandbars for shorebirds during spring and fall migration. In summer there is a large colony of Cliff Swallows under the bridge over the river.

At this point you can go back to K17 and turn left (south) to return to U.S. 54 after 10.5 miles, 5 miles west of where you first turned off this highway. Or you can cross the river and follow

the paved road for a little more than 2 miles beyond the bridge and turn right (south). Continue to follow the paved road as it works its way south, but watch for signs indicating other sections of the Cheney Wildlife Management Area where you can turn off and park to view the lake from the east shore and explore additional terrestrial habitats.

STAFFORD, KANSAS

Except when all waters are completely frozen, a visit to Quivira National Wildlife Refuge provides excellent opportunities for observing shorebirds and waterfowl as well as the species characteristic of the sand prairie. Continue east on u.s. 50 from the sign indicating the business district of Stafford for 6 miles to the town of Zenith. Turn left (north) here on a hard-surfaced township road and continue for 8 miles, the last mile of which is unpaved. Then turn right (east) at the Quivira sign and turn left on the second road to enter the headquarters area of the refuge. (Note: entrance into the headquarters is being changed so be alert for a slightly different route to begin this tour.) Follow this road past the area headquarters and along the east side of the Little Salt Marsh. From November through April watch for the Bald Eagle which winters in large numbers around this part of the refuge. The road then bears left across the north end of the Little Salt Marsh, crossing two low-water bridges that provide outflow for Rattlesnake Creek. You get the best view of open water from this end, so stop from time to time to scan the lake and investigate the stands of bullrush and cattails along the edge.

You eventually come to a good sand road; turn right. In 1.4 miles there is a stand of large cottonwoods to your left. Park along the road and take the opportunity to explore this more extensive area of deciduous woodland for the terrestrial species possible there. Return to your car and continue in the same direction. The road will jog right, left once, jog right, and then left again. After the last left turn, stop and check Park Smith Lake on your right for diving ducks during migration as well as for grebes, herons, and waterfowl during the summer. About 4 miles after turning onto this road you will intersect Stafford Co. 484. Continue north across this paved road onto a refuge road that takes you into the north end of the refuge.

This road goes through an area of sand prairie with open stands of cottonwoods and thickets of shrubs, marshes and shallow pools, and deeper ponds. During the summer in these habitats you can expect to see both species of kingbirds as well as Scissor-tailed Flycatchers, Brown Thrashers and Northern Mockingbirds, Loggerhead Shrikes, Bell's Vireos, Dickcissels, Lark

*The saline flats at Quivira, cracked by the heat, glitter in the bright
sunlight. How can the Snowy Plover and its young survive the rigors of
such a habitat?*

Sparrows, and birds associated with the marshes and ponds.
This habitat is also appropriate for migrants like Orange-
crowned Warblers, Yellow-rumped Warblers, and wintering passerines like Harris' Sparrows. After 3 miles you intersect an east-
west township road. Turn left (west) here and cross Rattlesnake
Creek. In about 1 mile stop the car and scan the mudflats to your
right (north) for concentrations of shorebirds during migration;
also check during the summer because large numbers of stragglers have not gone north and some birds are already heading
south again.

Then turn left at the "wildlife tour" sign onto a one-way loop
road that goes through the Big Salt Marsh. For most of the distance this road is on top of a dike and provides access to open
water, shallow pools, and marshy habitats. Although densities
of migrant shorebirds are often not as great as those at Cheyenne
Bottoms (see Great Bend KS), the variety is excellent, and because of the nature of the vegetation species like the American
Bittern are usually more visible. Nesting waterfowl include Canada Goose, Mallard, Gadwall, Northern Pintail, Blue-winged
Teal, Northern Shoveler, Redhead, and Ruddy Duck. Other

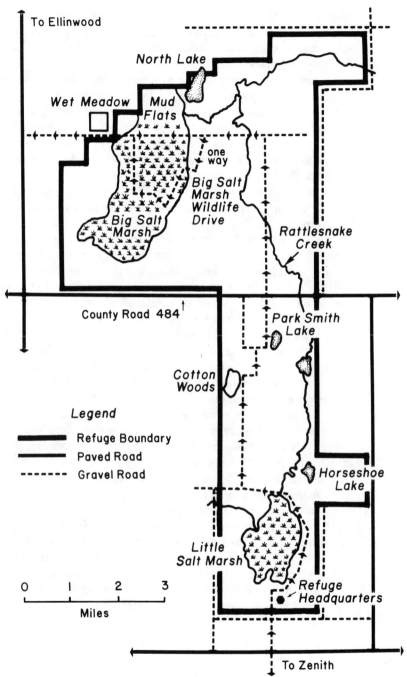

To Ellinwood

North Lake

Wet Meadow   Mud
Flats

one
way

Big Salt
Marsh
Wildlife
Drive

Big Salt
Marsh

Rattlesnake
Creek

County Road 484

Park Smith
Lake

Cotton
Woods

Legend

▬▬▬ Refuge Boundary
───── Paved Road
------- Gravel Road

Horseshoe
Lake

Little
Salt Marsh

0   1   2   3

Miles

Refuge
Headquarters

To Zenith

MAP 20. *Quivira National Wildlife Refuge Area*

nesting species of note are Eared and Pied-billed Grebes, White-faced Ibis, Northern Harrier, King, Sora, and Virginia Rails, American Avocet, Black-necked Stilt, Wilson's Phalarope, and Forster's and Black Terns.

As you go north on the dike to intersect the east-west township road again, you should drive slowly and stop from time to time to look for Snowy Plover on the road or in the shallow pools to your right. This is also a good place to search for Least Terns flying over the pools any time from mid-May through June and July. This location is the most important nesting site in Kansas for both the Snowy Plover and Least Tern so care should be made to minimize your disturbance. During the breeding season you should not leave the dike road, and the time you spend at this point in your tour should be minimal. When you reach the end of the dike road, stop and scan the mudflats to the north again. You can get closer to any concentrations of shorebirds by turning right here and then walking out on the roads to the oil well pads. Most of the wells are shut down now, and the roads are closed to vehicles; again be careful since the Snowy Plovers choose these raised areas for nest sites.

Go west on the township road for about 1 mile beyond where you turned off the dike road and stop. On your right (north) is a wet meadow where Bobolinks nest in May and June. Black Rails have also been seen here in July. Continue west on this road as it goes up a little in elevation and proceeds through a shelterbelt planting. During passerine migration check this area, and in the summer there is usually a pair of Mississippi Kites coasting above the trees. Swainson's Hawks are also quite common from mid-April until late summer. Eastern Screech-owls occur here throughout the year. You then leave the corner of the shelterbelt into an area of farmland and intersect a north-south paved road at 3.4 miles from where you turned off the dike road.

At this point you can turn left and reach Stafford 17 miles to the south. If you turn right, you can reach Ellinwood KS on u.s. 56 by going north for 4 miles to the Barton-Stafford County line, jogging right and then left before heading north again for another 5 miles. Turn right, less than 0.5 mile, then turn left, cross the Arkansas River, and enter Ellinwood.

CEDAR HILLS PRAIRIE

MEDICINE LODGE, KANSAS

The Red Hills or Gypsum Hills, as they are often called, are typ-
ified by a marked relief of exposed rocky slopes and rolling hills
with a striking, red clay soil. While geologically unique to southcentral Kansas, the Red Hills extend through central Oklahoma
to northern Texas. The native vegetation in the uplands is mixed-
grass prairie with an overstory of cedar forming a savannah-like
aspect. The major water courses are Elm Creek, which flows into
the Medicine Lodge River just south of the city, and the Salt Fork
of the Arkansas River, which also flows south into Oklahoma.
Scattered groves of cottonwoods, elms, hackberry, and bur oak
occur in these valleys. Except for Barber County State Fishing
Lake (just 0.8 mile north of town on u.s. 281), which should be
checked for waterfowl at appropriate seasons, there are no public areas in either Barber or Comanche counties notable for birding. Thus, this tour is a roadside excursion.

If the breeding-bird survey that begins near Coldwater is ex-
emplary of what you will find, then we suspect the approximately 120-mile circuit we describe will provide you with good
birding. This June census route regularly reports relatively large
numbers of Scissor-tailed Flycatchers, Bell's Vireos, and Lark
Sparrows. However, the more infrequently observed species—
Wild Turkey, Lesser Prairie-chicken, Burrowing Owl, Greater
Roadrunner, Black-headed Grosbeak, and Cassin's Sparrow as
well as the possible Carolina Chickadee and Painted Bunting—
will entice you on this trip.

To start this tour, drive south from Medicine Lodge on u.s. 281
along the eastern edge of the Gypsum Hills. Although the highway turns south at Hardtner, continue west on an all-weather
road. About 11 miles west of Hardtner the road curves south into
the valley of the Salt Fork of the Arkansas River. In spring, summer, and fall watch for Least Terns which nest along the Salt
Fork. You should also expect large numbers of Cliff Swallows,
since many of the bridges in this area support large nesting col-
onies. It would be worthwhile to check under any bridge you
cross; you might not only find swallow nests, but you might also
flush both Eastern and Say's Phoebes, using these sites for nests,
and often owls roosting during daylight hours. The road actually

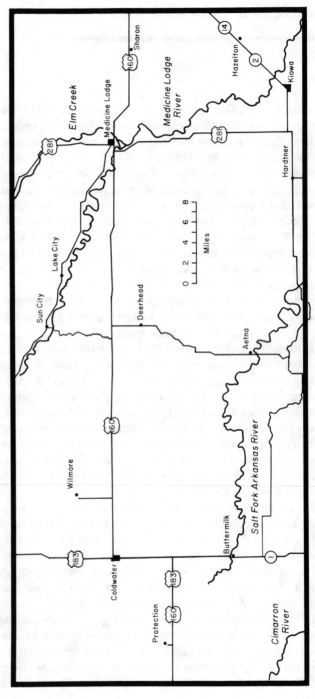

MAP 21. *Barber and Comanche Counties*

dips into Oklahoma beyond the river and becomes less suitable for travel in rainy and snowy weather since even graded gravel roads become "soupy" when wet in this part of the state. At the next road junction go north through Aetna and Deerhead to U.S. 160. Cassin's Sparrows have been reported from the Aetna area, and a prairie dog town between Aetna and Deerhead has had Burrowing Owls.

If you choose not to go north, continue west into Comanche County, stopping along the road wherever it appears the birding might be good. Carolina Chickadees and Painted Buntings might be found in brushy areas along arroyos. Keep especially alert for the Greater Roadrunner in this area. In fall and winter you will see flocks of American Robins, Eastern Bluebirds, and Mountain Bluebirds feeding on the cedar "berries." Careful inspection will also allow you to find an occasional Townsend's Solitaire. You will reach Highway K1 41 miles west of Hardtner. Turn north and continue for 14 miles to Coldwater. Just beyond the railroad tracks in Coldwater, turn left (west), go about 1.5 miles, turn left again, and continue south, recrossing the tracks, to reach Coldwater Lake. If waterfowl are present, you will be able to observe them from the road.

From Coldwater, follow U.S. 160 east back to Medicine Lodge. Another, shorter loop out of Medicine Lodge can be made northwest along the valley of the Medicine Lodge River to Sun City with a return south to U.S. 160 via a gravel road. This route will not get you into the heart of the cedar hill prairies, but there are many places to stop along the road and explore the riparian habitats. U.S. 281 north of Medicine Lodge skirts Elm Creek and finally crosses it about 8 miles north. Again these riparian habitats can be productive, especially during passerine migration.

MIXED-GRASS PRAIRIE

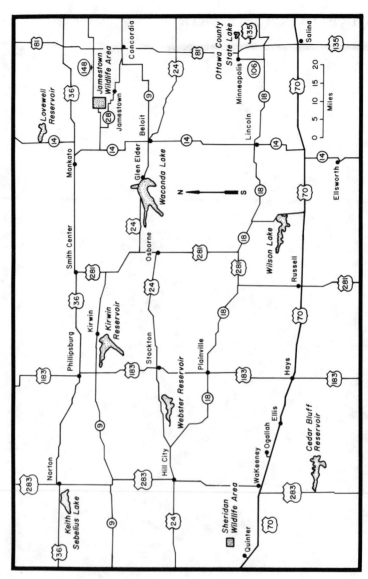

MAP 22. *Northern Mixed-grass Prairie*

GLEN ELDER, KANSAS

When the Glen Elder Dam was built across the Solomon River, the famous Waconda Springs near Cawker City disappeared under the waters of Waconda Lake, but this reservoir now provides some of the best fishing in Kansas as well as dependable waterfowl habitat for both spring and fall migrations.

To reach Glen Elder State Park on the north shore of the lake, proceed 0.7 mile west of Glen Elder on u.s. 24 and turn left into the park (permit required). Roads to the lake near the park entrance will provide access for waterfowl viewing near the dam. If you proceed west into the camping area, you will find other places to park and scan the middle part of the lake.

The park near Cawker City does not require a permit and provides access to the lake shore. Go 5.5 miles west of the state park entrance on u.s. 24 and turn left (south) and continue to the lake shore. Just 0.3 mile south of this corner, you can turn left onto an old hardtop road; this will eventually dead-end at the lake shore amid riparian willows and cottonwoods.

For a greater variety of terrestrial habitats as well as the shallower aquatic habitats attractive to waders and waterfowl, you should explore the upper end of the lake where much land has been set aside in the 12,500-acre Glen Elder Wildlife Management Area. To reach these areas, go 6.5 miles west from the state park entrance on u.s. 24 to the second blinker light in Cawker City. About 4 miles west of this light on u.s. 24 a dirt road to your left (south) continues to a parking area 0.6 mile from the highway. Just south of the parking area the North Fork of the Solomon River is bordered by a riparian forest of cottonwood, elm, honey locust, and silver maple. As you drive into this area notice the number of windbreak plantings, cultivated strips, and old fields, providing a variety of bird habitats that you should also explore on foot.

There is another dirt road to the south of u.s. 24 about 3 miles west of the blinker light. Turn left here and continue for 1 mile; park where the road turns to your left and spend some time on foot. The habitat is similar to that of the previously mentioned site, but you are farther from the riparian habitat.

The most productive survey of the wildlife area, however, can be made on a loop that begins with a left turn off U.S. 24 onto a gravel road 2.3 miles west of the blinker light, just beyond the bridge over Oak Creek. After you turn off the highway, stop and check the small lake to your left. Then continue south for 0.7 mile to a parking area off to your left where you can leave the car and walk through some oldfield and fencerow habitats. At 1.3 miles from the highway you come to a bridge over the North Fork of the Solomon River. A little beyond the bridge a road to your right goes to another parking area, and you can spend more time on foot. Not far beyond this point, the road becomes more dirt than gravel and may be impassable in wet weather. At 2.2 miles from the highway you cross the South Fork at another bridge, and then the road continues through areas of old fields and fencerows. At 5.4 miles stop the car along the road and walk to your right through a cultivated field to an old oxbow lake and marsh where you should expect herons and waterfowl at the appropriate seasons.

At 6 miles from the highway, take the left turn at the fork, turn left again in 0.6 mile, and continue past the stop sign onto the blacktop for 2 miles to a second stop sign. Turn left here toward Cawker City, continue north for 2.1 miles, and then turn right into another section of the wildlife area. At 0.8 mile from the corner, turn left toward the lake, drive as far as you can, and park. This access provides no views of open water, but it takes you to some narrow coves lined with cottonwoods and willows.

To reach more open water, return to the hardtop, turn right, proceed for just 0.1 mile, and then turn left onto a gravel road that goes down toward the water at the very upper end of the reservoir. This is a good area for a variety of waterfowl and waders. When you return to this turn-off, turn left (north) towards Cawker City and proceed across the causeway. Parking is limited on the causeway, but as you cross you will note two utility buildings on the right side of the road. You can pull off here to scan both sides of the causeway, including the marshy vegetation to the east. Sometimes during migration there are huge numbers of various waterfowl in view from this vantage point, but a spotting scope will be necessary to identify most of them. To complete this loop tour, continue on the causeway road to the blinker light in Cawker City, about 1.5 miles to the north.

JAMESTOWN, KANSAS

The Jamestown Wildlife Management Area contains a lake formed from the impoundment of Marsh Creek in Cloud and Republic counties, adjacent marshes, and a limited amount of upland areas. The best time to visit the area is during the spring waterfowl migration when both puddle ducks and divers are attracted to the open water. Fall migration is good, too, but since the area is hunted you should choose a time when the season is not open. Few waterfowl are in evidence during the summer months, although Mallard, Blue-winged Teal, and probably Wood Duck nest here. Nesting Yellow-headed Blackbirds, on the other hand, make their presence quite obvious. The upland areas have windbreaks of Russian olive, cedar, and honey locust, providing nesting habitat for Bell's and Warbling Vireos and Yellow Warblers.

To reach the marsh, turn north from K28 at Jamestown on an unmarked, hard-surfaced road. After 2.5 miles turn left (west) for 1 mile, then right (north) for 1 mile, and left again (west) for just about 1 mile where the road to your left leads to the south dam parking area, about 0.6 mile from this corner. This road along the east side of the lake provides the best access for waterfowl viewing. Return to the previous corner, continue for another 0.5 mile, and then turn left (west). Just before the road crosses a bridge, 0.4 mile from the corner, turn off to your right and continue to a parking area at the north dam site. Many cattails border the lake here, and this is a convenient place to park and explore the upland areas as well. A colony of Cliff Swallows also nests under the bridge.

164

Mixed-grass Prairie

The attraction of Buckner Valley State Park and the adjacent Hodgeman County Lake Park is the presence of perennial water sources from springs that permit the development of a good riparian woodland in the midst of the more arid environment along the western border of the mixed-grass prairie. During the breeding season, the characteristic birds of this habitat can be found here. Check the cottonwoods for Mississippi Kites, and expect both Northern (Bullock's) and Orchard Orioles as well as Western Kingbirds. Swainson's Hawks should be seen overhead during this season, while in the winter the soaring *buteos* will be Rough-legged and Ferruginous Hawks. A few Red-tails can be found at any season. The lake attracts migrating waterfowl, and you should search the riparian vegetation during spring and fall for migrant passerines with the very real expectation of finding vagrants from either the east or the west.

To reach this area take K156 west from Jetmore for almost 6 miles. The turn-off is on the south side of the highway, just after the road turns directly west again after angling southwest. The state park offers visitors scenic views of the picturesque Buckner Valley, and as you drive around the park during the breeding season, listen for Cassin's Sparrows. You may see a few "skylarking" in the rolling prairie areas, although at this very eastern edge of their range the populations fluctuate yearly.

KINGSDOWN, KANSAS

From this town on U.S. 54 in Ford County, just about half way
between Greensburg and Meade, take K94 south for 11 miles to
its end at Clark County State Fishing Lake and Wildlife Management Area. The lake, formed in the canyon of Bluff Creek, a
northern tributary of the Cimarron River, is located in one of the
most picturesque parts of the southern mixed-grass prairie. The
lake attracts a variety of waterbirds—ducks and geese, loons and
grebes, gulls and terns, and waders. Of note are Tundra Swans
that appear occasionally during the fall. The cottonwoods associated with the lake provide good habitat for birds, and the canyon walls that rise dramatically above the lake offer breeding
sites for Rock Wrens and suitable habitat for migrant sparrows
and other small passerines.

After entering the park, K94 turns south along the eastern
boundary and in about a mile turns west again to reach the lakeshore. At this point, a gravel road continues south and snakes
along around the top of the canyon but eventually drops down
to the dam. From the dam you can scan the entire south end of
the lake for waterfowl. Continue on this gravel road to the west;
then turn right in about 2 miles on gravel road that will take you
to the extreme northwest corner of the lake where an extensive
cattail marsh is worth checking. Return to the east side of the
lake the way you came. From K94, follow a gravel road to your
left, just as the highway turns east, to reach the north end of the
lake where you can cross the creek and take a nature trail.

One mile east of the park boundary on K94 the highway turns
north towards U.S. 54. If you have the time, turn right (south) at
this point and follow this gravel road south for 16 miles to Ashland. The annual breeding-bird survey conducted in June near
Ashland tallies relatively large numbers of Mississippi Kites and
Swainson's Hawks as well as many Lark and Cassin's Sparrows.
On this beautiful drive through the prairie in spring, fall, and
winter you will find longspurs and pipits in addition to the Western Meadowlarks and Horned Larks. Where this road crosses
Bluff Creek and its tributaries, check the trees for migrants in
spring and fall.

At Ashland, turn right (west) on U.S. 160. In 11 miles you

merge with U.S. 283 coming from the south; continue on U.S. 160 as it curves north. In 2 miles from this point you will be in the Big Basin and come to a turn-off to St. Jacob's Well. This Kansas Department of Wildlife and Parks site preserves an excellent stand of mixed-grass prairie where you can expect Grasshopper Sparrows and Dickcissels. Frankly, the birds take second place to the wildflowers, which are ablaze in color during the growing season at this well-watered natural sink. From here you can return to U.S. 54 at Minneola, 14.5 miles north on U.S. 283.

Dancing and swirling, flocks of Horned Larks enliven the stark, windswept winter landscape.

MANKATO, KANSAS

Besides providing excellent opportunities for observing waterfowl during the spring and fall migrations and in the winter as
long as the water stays open, Lovewell Reservoir provides a variety of habitats, including a few good stands of riparian oak and
hackberry forest, that make birding here at any season worth
your effort. For visitors from farther east, this is one of the most
easterly sites where you can regularly expect to find Black-billed
Magpies.

To reach the reservoir, go east from Mankato on u.s. 36 for
about 5 miles, then turn left (north) on K14, and continue for 9
miles. At this point turn right (east) on a dirt road, which should
not be used during or immediately after especially wet weather.
To reach the lower end of the reservoir under wet conditions
when this dirt road might be impassable, continue north for 1
more mile and turn right (east) on a gravel road. After 4 miles,
turn right (south) and continue for 1.5 miles to enter the Cedar
Point Area of Lovewell State Park (permit required). If weather
permits, turn off on the dirt road since it crosses several inlets
into the reservoir and skirts the northern edge of Lovewell Wildlife Management Area. Continue east of K14 on this dirt road for
0.7 mile and then turn right (south) on a road that parallels a
long inlet where Montana Creek flows into the reservoir. This
location is worth searching well since it can be especially good
for waterfowl, waders, and other waterbirds and species of riparian habitats, depending upon the season. Return to the east-
west dirt road, turn right, and continue eastward. As time
permits follow several other turn-offs on your right into the
Lovewell Wildlife Management Area, since they provide access
to excellent mixed-grass prairie, edge habitats of natural vegetation, and planted shelterbelts of cedar, Russian olive, and deciduous shrubs. The road also crosses several creeks flowing into
the reservoir on the north shore with good stands of riparian
vegetation along the banks.

Four miles from K14, turn right (south) on a gravel road which
enters the Cedar Point Area of Lovewell State Park in 0.5 mile.
The state park provides good access to the lower end of the reservoir for waterfowl viewing (permit required). Most of the ter-

Summer's heat smears the path of the dusty road west across the rolling prairie. Black-billed Magpies benefit from the ranch hand's late-night return from town.

restrial habitat in this area suffers from development, but there are small patches of natural vegetation, including some relatively dense stands of red cedar.

To reach the southern shore of the reservoir, leave the state park, turn right (east) at the first road, and continue for 1 mile; then turn right (south) on a road that takes you below the dam of the reservoir. After about 3 miles you will come to a crossroad; turn right (west). After 1.5 miles the road turns south for 1 mile and then turns west again. Continue on this road for 3 miles and turn right (north). You can get to this same point by going north on K14 for 5 miles from its intersection with u.s. 36 east of Mankato, turning right, continuing for 1 mile, and then turning left (north). Follow this road north through some nice stands of riparian oak and hackberry. This is private land, but birding can be satisfactory from the road. You then reach the south shore of the lake 3.3 miles from the turn-off. You should stop from time to time, not only to scan the reservoir for waterfowl but also to find birds in the riparian forest vegetation. At 4.7 miles from the turn-off, just after crossing a bridge, the road to your left enters the Oak Hill Area of Lovewell State Park. This is an undeveloped site, and no permit is required. Although this 0.5-mile loop can be driven in dry weather, it is better to walk it if you can since this gives you a greater chance of seeing a variety of both terrestrial and aquatic birds. Return to your car and follow the gravel road as it turns south away from the lake. After about 2.5 miles you will reach a stop sign. Turn right (west) and in 3 miles you will come to the junction with K14, 5 miles north of U.S. 36.

Mankato,
Kansas

MINNEAPOLIS, KANSAS

Mixed-grass Prairie

Although some waterfowl do use the 138-acre Ottawa County State Fishing Lake during migration, the surrounding 700 acres are more valuable throughout the year as a birding location because this park is an island of good deciduous forest surrounded by prairie in which such nesting species as Rose-breasted Grosbeak can be expected.

To reach this site go 4 miles east on K93 from the junction with U.S. 81 just east of Minneapolis. Continue on K93 as it bends left rather than taking the hard left that runs along the western boundary of the park. Drive carefully through the concession area and proceed towards the north end of the lake, stopping just beyond a low water bridge 1.2 miles from the entrance. You should explore the narrow, but well-developed riparian forest of cottonwoods and hackberry along both the east and west sides of this north inlet.

For better waterfowl viewing, as you approach the park continue straight ahead on the gravel road (Ottawa Co. 432) rather than turning into the park on K93. At 0.3 mile, turn left and drive into the park on a road that runs along the east shore of the lake. In a mile this road enters another area of riparian forest along the east inlet with many opportunities to park and walk about to find birds. Eventually this road comes to a stop sign; turn left here and then in 0.5 mile turn left again. This road continues to the north inlet, but watch for a gate on your left into the wildlife area where you can park and walk into a small tract of prairie.

NORTON, KANSAS

On the eastern edge of the High Plains within 15 miles of the Nebraska border, Keith Sebelius Lake is one the few relatively large bodies of water in this part of Kansas that can be expected to attract waterfowl during migration. Terrestrial vegetation is not especially varied, but there are plantings in the developed recreational areas and riparian woodlands along the margins of the lake where it narrows down to the valley of Prairie Dog Creek.

To reach this site, take U.S. 36 west out of Norton; 4.3 miles from the junction with U.S. 283 in Norton, turn left on K261 and enter the Leota Cove area of Prairie Dog State Park (permit required). Follow the road straight into the park, and at 0.8 mile past the park office you will come to a "T." For waterfowl viewing continue straight through the "T" on a dirt road leading to the lake shore, or turn left at the "T" and take any of the dirt roads leading off to your right towards the lake. The cottonwoods along the shore of the lake in this area provide cover for the typical birds of riparian woodlands, and they can be especially worthwhile to explore during passerine migration for errant warblers from both east and west.

Investigate less disturbed habitat by returning to U.S. 36 and turning left (west). Go 2 miles and then turn left again (south) on K383. Continue south for 3.5 miles, crossing the upper end of the lake, and then turn left into a section of the Norton Wildlife Management Area on a road that dead-ends in 0.4 mile. From here you can walk about, exploring the cottonwoods along the water and the nearby field and fencerow vegetation.

━━━━━━━━━━━━━━━━

172

_____

Mixed-grass
Prairie

Kirwin National Wildlife Refuge comprises more than 10,000 acres of mixed-grass prairie, riparian woodland, cropland, and open water formed by the damming of the North Fork of the Solomon River just downstream from its junction with Bow Creek. Water is more predictable during the spring migration than in the fall, and you can expect to see large numbers of Canada Geese, Greater White-fronted Geese, Mallards, and Northern Pintails, as well as Gadwalls, Green-winged Teals, Blue-winged Teals, American Wigeons, Northern Shovelers, and Common Mergansers. Later in the spring, Baird's Sandpipers, Long-billed Dowitchers, American Avocets, and Wilson's Phalaropes are common, but since shorebird habitat is sparse opportunities to see these migrants are limited. The fall waterfowl migration is also good, since usually enough water is available to attract a variety of waterbirds, including Western Grebes.

The well-developed riparian vegetation associated with the reservoir and the streams from which it was formed attracts a variety of passerines during both spring and fall migration. Although most of the warblers will be yellows, orange-crowned, and yellow-rumped, there is a real possibility of finding both eastern vagrants like Chestnut-sided and Magnolia Warblers and western vagrants like Townsend's and MacGillivray's Warblers.

As long as the water remains open in the winter, there will be a large population of Canada Geese and Mallards. Bald Eagles will be present, and eagle watching is popular with visitors. Also expect to see Golden Eagles and Ferruginous Hawks. A few waterfowl like Canada Goose and Mallard remain to nest. Other nesting species of note on the refuge are Double-crested Cormorant, Burrowing Owl, Black-billed Magpie, Orchard Oriole, and Dickcissel.

To reach the refuge, go south on u.s. 183 from Phillipsburg for 5 miles from the intersection with u.s. 36. Then turn left (east) on K9 at Glade, continue east past the sign indicating the road to the refuge for approximately 9 miles from u.s. 183, and then turn right (south) just before reaching the town of Kirwin, a little over a mile father east. You immediately come to a ork; make a right turn, enter the refuge, bear left at the next road junction, and

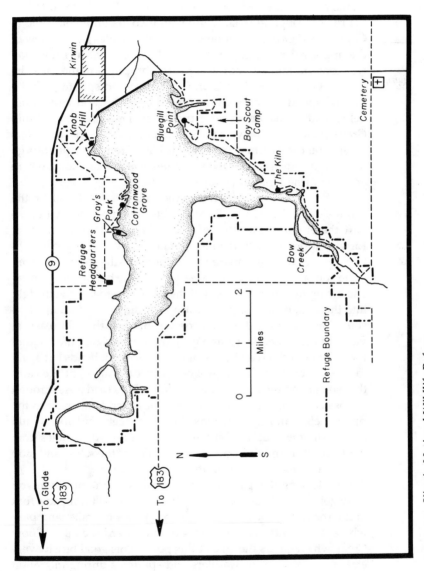

MAP 23. *Kirwin National Wildlife Refuge*

follow the signs to Knob Hill, which you will reach after 0.8 mile from K9. This point will afford a good view of the lower end of the reservoir. The terrestrial vegetation here is grassland with clumps of cottonwoods in the draws and a few scattered cedars. Continue on this gravel road until you come to a stop sign about 1 mile beyond the rest rooms at Knob Hill. Turn left and follow the road through grassland and cottonwoods until you come to Cottonwood Grove, a camping area that provides a good view of the upper reservoir, 1.2 miles from the stop sign. In 1 mile you will come to another stop sign; turn abruptly left and take the road to Gray's Park. This is an especially good spot to park the car and spend some time exploring the cottonwood groves, old fields, and croplands for terrestrial birds. From the turn-off into Gray's Park continue west for 1 mile to the refuge headquarters where you can obtain a map and bird list. From headquarters go north and return to K9, about 3 miles west of the point where you first turned into the refuge.

The best terrestrial habitat is in the valley of Bow Creek on the south side of the refuge. To reach this area, proceed east on K9 past the entrance into the refuge to the road into the town of Kirwin, approximately 10 miles from U.S. 183. Turn right (south) here, go around the square in the center of the town, and continue south below the dam, crossing a bridge below the spillway and swinging around the end of the dam. The road on your right into the refuge has a sign indicating the direction of Camp Hanson. Continue past this road for 3.8 miles, turn right (east) at Pleasant Ridge Cemetery, and go 4 miles; turn right onto another road just after the road bends right and before it bends left again to cross over Bow Creek. A small sign on your right indicates that you are on the road to the "the kiln." This road goes through a mosaic of mixed-grass prairie and cultivated fields next to the riparian elms and cottonwoods along the creek, and you should stop from time to time to bird interesting spots. At 2.5 miles from the turn-off, turn left into a parking area at "the kiln," and stop to search on foot for birds in the various habitats.

After leaving this parking area, continue in the direction you were going. At about 1.5 miles farther on you will come to a fork in the road; take the left branch, continue for 0.6 mile, and park where the road turns right. Walk down toward the inlet of Bow Creek which enters the lake at this point. This good brushy vegetation is excellent for warblers and sparrows during migration and provides habitat for those passerine species that remain for the winter.

Return to your car and continue on. At 0.5 mile beyond this corner you reach a road coming in from the left and then one from the right, but continue straight through this crossroads. In 0.2 mile turn left on a road, just before reaching the entrance to a private trailer park, and then right to Bluegill Point for an excellent view of the lake. Return to the crossroads, turn left, and continue past the entrance to Camp Hanson toward the dam. In 1.3 miles a loop road to your left provides another opportunity to scan the lake for waterfowl. At 0.7 mile from this turn-off, you will come to the hardtop road just south of the end of the dam; turn left (north) to return to K9 through the town of Kirwin.

Mixed-grass
Prairie

At the western extremity of the mixed-grass prairie, the Sheridan Wildlife Management Area provides a riparian oasis along the banks of the Saline River northeast of Quinter in Gove County, just a few miles off I-70. During the summer in the box elders and cottonwoods that follow the margins of the river you can expect to find Northern and Orchard Orioles, Warbling Vireos, a few Red-eyed Vireos, House Wrens, Black-capped Chickadees, Northern Flickers, and Red-bellied Woodpeckers. This island of trees in the prairie should also attract numerous passerines during migration. Although the forested habitat provides little winter food, the weedy growth in the bed of the former lake here should be good for the expected species of wintering sparrows, like American Tree Sparrows, White-crowned Sparrows, and Harris' Sparrows.

To reach this site, leave I-70 at Exit 107, and go north on K212 into Quinter on Main Street. At the end of Main Street, turn right on old U.S. 40 and proceed east for 2.8 miles. Then turn left (north) on Gove County 515. This road passes through cultivated land and excellent stands of mixed-grass prairie. In summer you should find Lark Buntings, Horned Larks, and Lark Sparrows along this road, and in winter, longspurs. After 5.3 miles, turn left onto the road along the wildlife area. You can park near the old dam site and explore upstream or go a little farther west to a well-constructed rock shelter house where you can park and spend some time walking in the riparian habitat and adjacent prairie. There is a small cattail marsh farther up the road that might be worth visiting if you have the time.

RUSSELL, KANSAS

Like the Flint Hills to the east, the Smoky Hills of central Kansas with their outcrops of Dakota sandstone provide a picturesque setting for Wilson Lake, a U.S. Army Corps of Engineers impoundment with approximately 9,000 acres of surface. Birding around Wilson Lake can be very productive at any season given both the diverse habitats and the mix of eastern and western species. When approaching from the east on I-70, exit at K232 (milepost 206) and proceed about 10 miles north to the dam and Sylvan Park area (see below). When approaching from the west on I-70, continue about 8 miles east of the junction with U.S. 281 in Russell and exit at Bunker Hill (milepost 193). Go north on the unmarked but hardtop Bunker Hill–Luray Road for 4.2 miles and turn right (east) onto a gravel road through uplands of excellent mixed-grass prairie. At 2.4 miles from this turn-off you will come to the edge of the Wilson Wildlife Management Area around Spring Creek with its mix of prairie, cultivated fields, old fields, and riparian woodlands. In summer Dickcissels, Western Meadowlarks, and Grasshopper Sparrows are common in the prairie, and Upland Sandpipers can usually be found. Common breeding species in edge habitats include Great Horned Owl, both Eastern and Western Kingbirds, Blue Jay, Black-capped Chickadee, House Wren, Northern Mockingbird, Brown Thrasher, Loggerhead Shrike, and Lark Sparrow. In winter there are large flocks of Harris' and American Tree Sparrows.

At 2.8 miles from the Bunker Hill–Luray Road enter the wildlife area through a cattle guard. If the weather has been extremely wet, proceed with caution since the road soon becomes more sand and dirt than gravel. At 0.6 mile from the cattle guard you come to a fork in the road. The right fork takes you along the edge of the upper end of Wilson Lake. During March and again in October there are thousands of ducks and geese on the lake; especially notable are large concentrations of Redheads, Lesser Scaups, Mallards, and Northern Pintails, which are later followed by American White Pelicans, Franklin's Gulls, and American Coots. In late March, large flocks of Sandhill Cranes can often be seen flap-soaring high above the lake. The left-hand fork follows Cedar Creek and soon dead-ends close to the point where the Saline River flows into the lake. About 0.5 mile from the fork, take the road to the left and return to the Bunker Hill–Luray Road in 2.5 miles. When you reach the hardtop, turn right (north), cross the bridge over the Saline River, and then turn right on a dirt road 1.9 miles north of where you turned onto the hardtop. This road drops into the riparian habitats along the river, and the birds characteristic of this habitat include Orchard Oriole, Yellow Warbler, and Warbling Vireo in summer and a great variety of passerines during migration. A large colony of Cliff Swallows nests under the bridge.

Return to the hardtop, turn right (north) for 1.2 miles, and then turn right (east) onto a gravel road. At both 1 and 2 miles from this turn, roads to your right (south) go a short distance into the Wilson Wildlife Management Area on the north side of the river. Continue east on this gravel road to a stop sign at 4.7 miles; 1 mile beyond this stop sign a road to your right provides good access to the north shore of the lake for waterfowl viewing and riparian and shelterbelt habitats within the wildlife area. There is another road to the north shore of the lake at 3 miles from the stop sign. At 11.6 miles from the Bunker Hill–Luray Road you intersect highway K232; turn right (south) for 1.4 miles and turn right again to enter the Lucas Park area. The first road to your left provides opportunities for waterfowl viewing just behind the dam and returns you to K232 in 1.5 miles. If you continue straight, turn right 0.5 mile beyond this intersection and then turn right again in 1.7 miles on a gravel road to the swimming area. In summer, check the thickets of sandhill plum, rough-leaved dogwood, and aromatic sumac for Bell's Vireos and Blue Grosbeaks. And the open habitat of Lucas Park is often frequented in winter by flocks of Mountain Bluebirds. Before you get to the swimming area, however, turn right in 0.3 mile on a narrow sand road to the Rocktown Cove area where from early April until late September you can find Rock Wrens and Say's Phoebes in the outcrops of Dakota sandstone along the lake. Turkey Vultures often nest among these rocks. Since this road may not be suitable for some cars, proceed with caution; in fact, it might be more rewarding to walk in.

Return to K232 and cross the dam. Just beyond (east) the dam, turn left on K181, then immediately turn left again into the Sylvan Park area, and follow the signs to the Burr Oak Nature Trail parking area. Walk the jeep trail from the parking area, past the small cattail marsh, eventually coming to a sign indicating the boundary of the Wilson Wildlife Management Area. The riparian

*On the slope above you the Rock Wren scampers out on a ledge of Dakota
sandstone to observe your passing.*

habitat in the old channel of the Saline River is especially worth
your effort to explore. Besides edge species previously mentioned, permanent residents here include Northern Bobwhite,
Belted Kingfisher, Red-bellied Woodpecker, Black-billed Magpie,
American Kestrel, and Red-tailed Hawk. Rough-winged Swallows and occasionally a Common Barn-owl nest in the steep
banks of the old river channel north of this area. In winter, the
marshy areas along the nature trail and in the old river channel
often harbor Wilson's Snipe and Marsh Wren.

Return to K232 and turn left; 3 miles from the junction with
K181 turn right onto South Shore Drive. Just before you cross the
Hell Creek bridge with its large colony of Cliff Swallows, turn
left on the road to the Otoe Park area to reach the lake for waterfowl viewing. From early December until early March there is a
large wintering population of Bald Eagles around the lake; birds
can be seen perched on the ice near open water or in the trees
along the shore. They usually roost in a stand of dead cottonwoods in Deer Run Cove west of Otoe Park on the south shore
of the lake.

To reach Wilson State Park (permit required), return to the South Shore Drive and continue west to the turn-off into the park, 1.5 miles from K232. Access to the south shore of the lake can also be reached by continuing 5.7 miles farther west on South Shore Drive and turning right to Minooka Park. In winter the lake is usually ice-free until mid-January, and thousands of Common Mergansers occur along with large numbers of Common Goldeneyes and Mallards. Careful checking of these large flocks usually produces a variety of other waterfowl, including Canada Goose, Green-winged Teal, Gadwall, American Wigeon, Redhead, Bufflehead, and Hooded Merganser. In the uplands anywhere around the lake during the winter you have an excellent chance of seeing Rough-legged Hawk, Prairie Falcon, and an occasional Ferruginous Hawk. If you continue west on South Shore Drive from the junction with the road into Minooka Park, you return to Bunker Hill in about 7 miles. You can get back to I-70 at milepost 199 by going 3 miles to the south of the junction of South Shore Drive and the road to Minooka Park, 1.5 miles from K232.

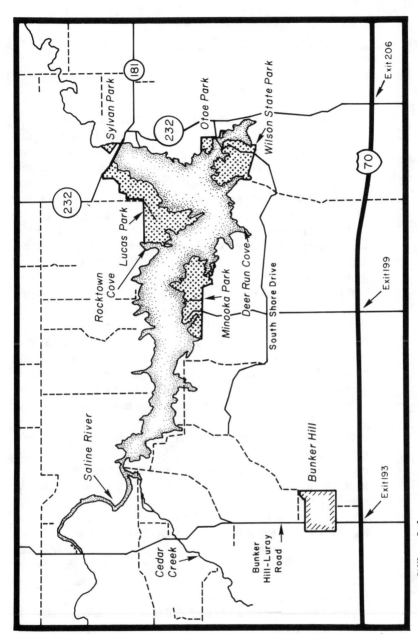

MAP 24. *Wilson Lake.*

The mixed-grass prairie and riparian woodland in the valley of the South Fork of the Solomon River in the Webster Wildlife Management Area and on the north shore of Webster Reservoir will provide productive birding throughout the year. Not only will you find the expected seasonally resident birds, but during migration you should expect the unexpected since this site lies just thirty minutes east of the 100th meridian, the biogeographic dividing line of the continent between east and west. The open waters of the lake offer waterfowl viewing during migration; some water birds, like the American White Pelican, linger on into summer.

From the intersection of u.s. 183 and u.s. 24 in Stockton, proceed west out of town on u.s. 24 for 9 miles and turn left into Webster State Park, Rock Point Area (permit required). Turn off the entrance road into the picnic area to view the lower end of the reservoir just above the dam, or follow the entrance road toward the park office, paralleling the north shore, and stop to scan the lake for waterfowl. The park office is 1.8 miles from the entrance, and, if you continue into the camping area, you can get a good view of the upper end of the lake.

Return just past the park office and make a hard left on a gravel road which goes back to u.s. 24 in 1.7 miles. To explore more diverse and less disturbed terrestrial habitats, turn left from this gravel road onto the first road to your left at 0.9 mile from the corner, bear right at a fork in 0.7 mile from the point where you turned left, and enter the Webster Wildlife Management Area after 1.2 miles. In this area of mixed-grass prairie the display of gaillardia during late May is impressive. Additionally plantings of Russian olive, cedar, and mulberry form windbreaks, supplementing the riparian cottonwood habitat in the floodplain of the river.

At 1.3 miles from the Webster Wildlife Area sign you come to a fork in the road. A left turn here takes you down onto the lower floodplain, but proceed with caution if the weather has been wet. This road exits the wildlife area about 1 mile from the fork. If you make a right turn here onto a gravel road you skirt the western edge of the wildlife area and can stop occasionally to explore on foot inviting habitats. Eventually you come to a hard-top road running north from the town of Damar; turn right (north) and return to U.S. 24, a little over 9 miles west of the state park entrance. If you take the right fork, you proceed through upland mixed-grass prairie, leaving the wildlife area 1.4 miles from the fork and returning to U.S. 24 in 0.8 mile, 4.3 miles west of the point where you first entered the state park.

There is another access to the Webster Wildlife Management Area approximately 3 miles west (7.3 miles west of the state park entrance) on U.S. 24. Turn left here, and about 1.5 miles from the point where you turned off the highway you enter an excellent riparian woodland of tall cottonwoods; stop and investigate the immediate area for birds. At 2.3 miles you leave the wildlife area. Turn left at the first intersection and return to U.S. 24 in 0.6 mile, just east of the point where you first began this loop.

*Stockton,
Kansas*

━━━━━━━━━

*Mixed-grass
Prairie*

One of the greatest advantages of birding at Cedar Bluff Reservoir is the absence of people. It does not have a good reputation as a fishing lake so the birds have the water much to themselves; the state park on the south shore has not been heavily used and has returned to the natural vegetation over much of the developed area. A second advantage is the surrounding area's heavy agricultural use; hence, the habitats around the reservoir contained in the more than 8,000 acres of the Cedar Bluff Wildlife Management Area form an oasis in a wheat desert. Apparently this is especially true in the winter, when many species find suitable cover in the riparian vegetation between the lake shore and the bluffs that give the reservoir its name. Large numbers of sparrows and finches occur along with Black-billed Magpies, Long-eared Owls, and occasionally Northern Shrikes. During spring and fall, the lake attracts the expected diversity of waterfowl, waders, and shorebirds, while migrant passerines frequent the willows, cottonwoods, shelterbelt plantings, and upland mixed-grass prairie.

To reach Cedar Bluff Reservoir, proceed south on U.S. 283 from exit 127 on I-70 in WaKeeney. Continue for 15 miles, keeping alert in winter for flocks of Horned Larks and longspurs and the Prairie Falcons associated with them. Then turn left (east) onto a dirt road to reach one section of the wildlife area. At 1.3 miles from this corner turn right onto a trail that cuts through sparse prairie heavily invaded by yucca and then skirts the cottonwood belt along the Smoky Hill River. This loop trail returns you to the township road in 1.6 miles, just 0.8 mile east of where you first entered.

Make a left turn here, return to U.S. 283, turn left (south), and drive only 0.6 mile to a turn-off on your right where you should park. Walk through the opening in the fence and explore the riparian habitat and associated uplands on the north side of the Smoky Hill River.

Return to your car, cross the river, and then turn left (east) on a sand road just 0.1 mile from the south end of the bridge. This is the best section in Cedar Bluff Wildlife Management Area for birding, and you should stop frequently to bird as the road winds its way in and out of the cottonwoods along the river or near the bluff or on top in good mixed-grass prairie. There are several convenient places to park, and you can walk through areas for a more thorough search for birds. In about 5 miles you leave the wildlife area and come to a yield sign on a major east-west township road at 6 miles. Turn right (west) here and return to u.s. 283 in 3 miles.

However, to reach the lake you should turn left (east); after 3.7 miles turn left (north) onto a paved road that initially enters another section of the wildlife area but eventually goes into the south shore area of Cedar Bluff State Park. As you drive north on this road, stop and listen for Rock Wrens in the draws on your left or park and walk the draws as they continue on your right to reach the riparian vegetation in the basin on the south arm of the reservoir. At 1 mile from the corner you enter the state park (permit required). Take any road that offers a view of the open water or brings you close to the extensive riparian vegetation that has grown up in the basin of the reservoir which no longer receives sufficient water to fill. Bell's Vireos are especially abundant in this habitat, but expect a variety of other nesting species characteristic of this habitat just east of the edge of the High Plains, like Bullock's (Northern) Orioles. In addition to riparian vegetation, there are shelterbelt plantings and good mixed-grass prairie.

Return to the park entrance and turn left (east). In 3.5 miles you reach k147. Turn left and proceed north. At 6.4 miles you come to the road into the north shore area of the Cedar Bluff State Park where development has greatly affected the habitat and access to the water for waterfowl viewing is limited. Continue for another 13 miles to reach I-70 at exit 135 in Ogallah.

SANDSAGE PRAIRIE AND SHORT-GRASS PRAIRIE

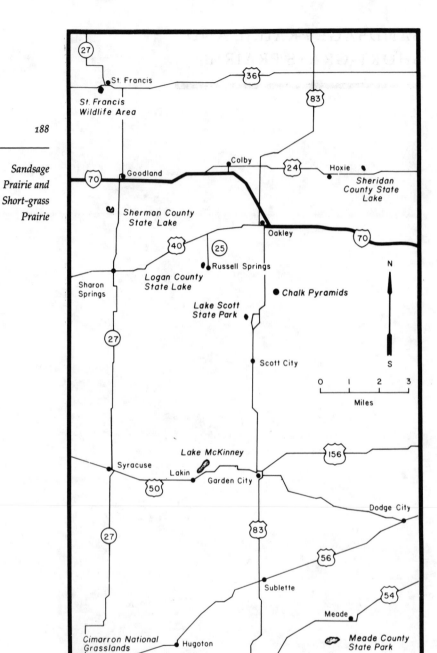

MAP 25. *Sandsage Prairie and Short-grass Prairie*

During the drought of the thirties many farms in Morton County in the extreme southwestern corner of Kansas were "dusted out," and the affected lands were eventually set aside for reclamation as part of the Cimarron National Grasslands. Extensive upland areas no longer cultivated have now returned to sandsage prairie, but good stands of riparian woodland stretch along the Cimarron River. Since both habitats attract species not easily found anywhere else in Kansas, a trip to Morton County is a rewarding excursion for area birders any time of the year. Visitors should stop at the office of the U.S. Forest Service in Elkhart to pick up an area map as well as a checklist prepared for the grasslands.

In Elkhart, you should stop at the cemetery in the northeast part of town, especially during migration when the habitat attracts flycatchers, vireos, and warblers and in winter when passerines down from the high country, like Mountain Chickadees, can often be discovered in the conifer plantings. The cemetery is also a good spot for wintering Merlins. Immediately north of the cemetery is the Elkhart City Dump with three settling ponds that attract waterfowl, corvids, and mixed species flocks of blackbirds. This is one of the most probable places to find the Chihuahuan Raven. In winter a stop at the airport in the southeast part of town can usually turn up Short-eared Owls and flocks of longspurs that should be carefully searched for species other than the abundant Lapland Longspur. Since the town is a wooded island on the high plains, it is worth some time just walking the residential streets, whether during breeding season or migration. In winter, especially if you locate a bird feeder, Scrub Jay, Curvebilled Thrasher, Bushtit, and Mountain Chickadee are possibilities.

The focal point for a tour of the Cimarron National Grasslands is the Forest Service campground on the Cimarron River. To reach this site, proceed north out of Elkhart on K27. About 2.5 miles north of town you come to the Soil Conservation Service Headquarters on the east (right) side of the highway. Even if the gate is closed, there is room to park on the shoulder of the road, and you can spend some time searching the large conifer plantings. In the winter months there will be juncos, House Finches, White-crowned and Harris' Sparrows, and Townsend's Solitaires. These species in turn attract accipiters and Merlins. The Great Horned Owl is a possibility at any time of year.

Continue north on κ27. During the summer large numbers of Cassin's Sparrows along the highway share the grasslands with Grasshopper Sparrows and Lark Buntings. Watch for an occasional Scissor-tailed Flycatcher on the wires and Dickcissels in the weedier spots. This stretch of the highway is also good for raptors in the winter; expect Red-tailed Hawk, Rough-legged Hawk, Ferruginous Hawk, Prairie Falcon, Merlin, and Northern Harrier. Also in the winter, especially if there has been a recent snowfall, thousands of Horned Larks and Lapland Longspurs will be along the road. The longspur flocks should be carefully checked since McCown's and Chestnut-collared Longspurs are also present.

At 7.5 miles north of Elkhart you come to the bridge over the Cimarron River. Just before reaching the bridge, turn right (east) into the campground and park. The river flows more-or-less from west to east, and the riparian vegetation is an avenue of approach to the Front Range for many migrants in the spring, like Western Wood-pewee and Lazuli Bunting, as well as a funnel for montane species invading the lowlands during severe winter weather. In the breeding season there are Northern (Bullock's) and Orchard Orioles here, and you can see Mississippi Kites floating overhead. At night, you can hear Common Poorwills calling, and the Common Barn-owl has appeared more regularly in recent years. As you walk along the river through the larger stands of cottonwoods, be alert for Ladder-backed Woodpecker, Wild Turkey, and Black-billed Magpie at any time of year. A small herd of elk also occurs in these bottomlands.

Just south of the campground entrance a road runs east from κ27, paralleling the Cimarron River. This is an all-weather road, but watch for drifted sand if your car has low clearance. Scaled Quail are usually seen along the roadside, and in winter check the large cottonwoods near the river for Golden and Bald Eagles. At 4.5 miles east of κ27 at several ponds on the north side of the road you can expect to find herons, waterfowl, and an occasional "peep." In all but the most severe winters, Marsh Wrens should be present. It is also worthwhile to spend some time exploring the riparian border beyond these ponds.

At 6.5 miles from κ27 you come to at "T"; turn right (south) and proceed 2.5 miles, then turn left (east), and continue for 1.5

The shed is long unused. The builder now entertains his grandchildren in Fresno. But the Scaled Quail finds the old homestead to its liking in the reclaimed lands of southwestern Kansas.

miles. At this point turn left (north) across a cattle guard and drive for about 0.5 mile to an oil pumping facility and park. To your north you should be able to see an observation blind placed at the edge of a Lesser Prairie-chicken booming ground. This is probably the best place in the United States to find the Lesser Prairie-chicken, and using the blind is the best way to see them. Contact the Forest Service office in Elkhart to find out if the blind is available for your use and plan to be in the blind at least one-half hour before sunrise. This species booms for a longer period of the year than does the Greater Prairie-chicken, and their booms are quite different, more like a bubbling sound. But even if you are here in the summer it is worth some time walking over these hills of sandsage prairie in hopes of flushing the chickens as well as finding Scaled Quail, Cassin's Sparrow, and Lark Bunting. In fall and winter, it is better strategy to locate the nearest milo field and visit the area in early morning or late afternoon observing the chickens as they fly into or out of these fields for feeding. In fall, winter, and early spring these sandsage hills are also the prime habitat for Chestnut-collared and McCown's Longspurs.

For another worthwhile tour from the campground, cross the

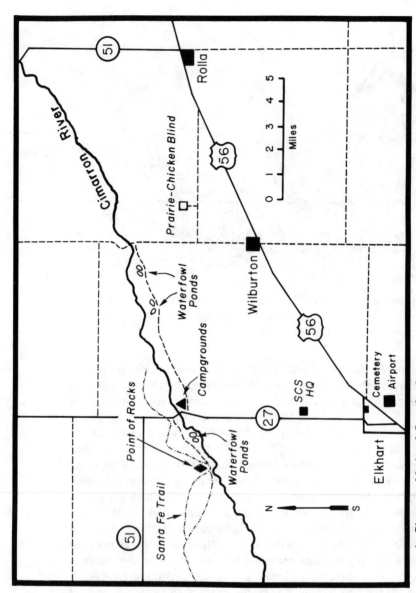

MAP 26. *Cimarron National Grasslands*

Cimarron River on K27 and then turn left (west) immediately north of the bridge, crossing a cattle guard on a dirt road that follows the Cimarron River west to Point of Rocks. About 1 mile from K27 a series of ponds can be reached by a road to a parking lot where you can stop and spend some time on foot. Besides waterbirds at the appropriate seasons, in winter the margins of these ponds are especially good for mixed species flocks of sparrows. You will have no trouble locating Point of Rocks, since it has served as a landmark for visitors since the days of the Santa Fe Trail. Be sure to look for the wagon ruts in the valley, still visible from the top of this outcrop of the Ogallala Formation. These rocky slopes provide the only habitat in Kansas for such southwestern species as Rufous-crowned Sparrow and Brown Towhee. Several pairs of Rock Wrens occur during the breeding season, and during migration check the shrubs on the slopes for warblers such as Blackpoll, Wilson's, and especially Mac-Gillivray's as well as Green-tailed Towhee.

Return to K27 and turn left and proceed 4 miles north to a paved road that runs west to Colorado. Turn left and drive for 2 miles or so, checking the pastures for Lark Bunting and Long-billed Curlew from spring to early fall. The curlew's melodic "ccoorrrrr-lee-yoo" is the signature sound of the short-grass plains and will not soon be forgotten. In winter months this area is good for larks and longspurs, often occurring as large "clouds" of birds rolling across the fields. During the breeding season in Morton County wherever you notice even a single cholla cactus, you should stop and investigate; in this area the plant is the preferred nest site of the Curve-billed Thrasher. If you continue west on K51 you eventually enter Baca County, Colorado, and the Comanche National Grasslands.

*Sandsage
Prairie and
Short-grass
Prairie*

Located at the junctions of K156, U.S. 50, and U.S. 83, Garden City has a few sites worth inspection by the visiting birder. The Lee Richardson Zoo in Finnup Park at the intersection of Main and Maple streets has a large stand of cottonwoods augmented by ornamental plantings. Not only will you find resident House Finches and nesting Mississippi Kites, but the vegetation attracts a variety of migrants in spring and fall. Although stocked with exotic species, the waterfowl pond at the zoo brings in native waterfowl as well, especially in winter. For several years there has been a nesting colony of Black-crowned Night-herons here. From the zoo, go south on Business U.S. 83 for 0.1 mile to the Arkansas River crossing. Although trees are sparse along this stretch of the river, extensive weedy fields here provide excellent cover and food for sparrows during the winter. In areas of sandsage prairie near the city, you can expect to find nesting Cassin's and Lark Sparrows, and perhaps Scaled Quail and Lesser Prairie-chicken, too.

HOXIE, KANSAS

A good riparian stand of cottonwoods below the dam at Sheridan County State Fishing Lake attracts a variety of birds to this impoundment on the north side of the Sand Creek valley, especially during the periods of passerine migration. Furthermore, a number of rock ledges provide nesting habitat for Rock Wrens. The lake is just about 80 acres in size, but a few waterfowl stop during migration.

To reach this site, go east on u.s. 24 from the junction with k23 in Hoxie for 11.2 miles. Then turn left (north) and continue for 0.5 mile to the park entrance on your right. If you follow this road, you completely circle the lake in about 3 miles, and it gives you the opportunity to stop and explore wherever the habitat looks inviting.

LAKIN, KANSAS

Just northeast of this town in Kearny County, Lake McKinney has water in most years; thus, it is an important habitat for waterbirds in the generally arid High Plains. Waterfowl can be seen here in every month of the year, unless the lake is completely frozen. But even then, a visit could be productive since Bald Eagles roost in the cottonwoods that border the lake. During the periods of waterfowl migration the greatest variety of birds will be seen. During March and April and again in late September and October, large numbers of Canada, Snow, and Greater White-fronted Geese use the lake for feeding and resting. There will also be a variety of both puddle ducks and divers among the geese, and expect loons, grebes, and American White Pelicans as well. In March and October, Sandhill Cranes can be found in nearby fields, or, at the very least, migrating overhead.

To reach the lake, travel 3 miles east of Lakin on U.S. 50 and than turn left (north) at milepost 47 onto a gravel road. Although access to this privately-owned lake is restricted, you can see most of the lake by following this gravel road. About 1 mile beyond this turn-off from U.S. 50, the highway crosses streams flowing (sometimes) toward the lake. Because a good stand of cattails is associated with these streams, a stop along the highway to check for a variety of marsh birds, including herons and rails, is worthwhile.

Another stop along U.S. 50 is the cemetery, which could offer some good birding during migration as well as in winter because of the conifer plantings. This site is about a quarter mile east of town on the north side of U.S. 50.

Just 0.1 mile west of the cemetery entrance is a hardtop road running south from U.S. 50. If you take this road you come to the Lakin Sewage Treatment Plant and the large pond associated with it. During migration this should offer ducks with an occasional gull, tern, or wader.

As is true elsewhere in western Kansas, a highway river crossing is worth exploring during periods of passerine migration. To reach the floodplain of the Arkansas River with its cottonwoods and salt cedars (Tamarisk), take K25 south for about 1.5 miles from its intersection with U.S. 50 in the center of Lakin.

LIBERAL, KANSAS

Several sites around this town on the Oklahoma–Kansas border are worth taking the short time necessary to investigate for birds. Because of its association with the city's wastewater treatment plant, McCoid Lake usually has sufficient water, even in summer, to attract a variety of waterfowl, and it remains open in the winter as well. Although the migration periods and winter offer the most promise, summer can be suprisingly good with American Avocet, Lesser Yellowlegs, Wilson Phalarope, and Black Tern among the species expected then. To reach McCoid Lake, go north from the intersection of U.S. 54 and U.S. 270/83 in the center of town, then turn right on Eighth Street, and proceed for 1.5 miles.

Another site near the center of town is the Seward County Sanitary Landfill at the junction of Truck Route U.S. 83 and U.S. 54. The refuse often attracts large numbers of birds, especially mixed species flocks of Brewer's and Yellow-headed Blackbirds and occasionally Great-tailed Grackles. Chihuahuan Ravens are also a possibility during most of the year.

If you drive northeast on U.S. 54, you come to a Roadside Park on your left about 9 miles from Liberal where the highway crosses the Cimarron River. The riparian border of cottonwoods and willows provides a migratory corridor out of the mountains in the fall as well as a pathway west in the spring. As a result, this site provides birders with an excellent opportunity to walk the river and check for migrants, not only western species like Orange-crowned Warblers and Audubon's Yellow-rumped Warblers but eastern stragglers like American Redstarts and Rose-breasted Grosbeaks. Usually a pair of Mississippi Kites is in residence each summer, and it's a good place for Orchard Orioles. At 3.5 miles farther northeast on U.S. 54, turn right on a hard-top county road that goes to Meade County State Park (see Meade KS).

A last possibility out of Liberal, especially if you are heading west, is to take U.S. 270/83 north to where U.S. 270 turns west with K51 and continues towards Hugoton. In spring, summer, and fall, check the mixed flocks of larks and long-spurs for Chestnut-collared and McCown's Longspurs that should be present in good numbers. At these times of year this is also a good landscape for Red-tailed, Rough-legged, and Ferruginous Hawks, Prairie Falcons, Merlins, and Golden Eagles.

MEADE, KANSAS

Because permanent bodies of water are always at a premium in the prairie regions of western Kansas, Lake Meade and the associated terrestrial habitats of Meade County State Park (permit required) are quite attractive to birds. If you visit the area between April and September, you will see Mississippi Kites nesting in the cottonwoods around the lake. Don't be too surprised to be serenaded in the evening by Chuck-will's-widows, which reach their most western distribution here, or to wake up to the gobbling of Wild Turkeys. During the spring and fall migrations, there can be impressive numbers of passerines, since the park is an oasis in a treeless area under heavy cultivation.

To reach the park take K23 south from Meade for 8 miles, and follow this highway as it runs west for another 5 miles to the park entrance. For the best view of the lake, take the 1.5-mile drive that follows the lakeshore along the south, east, and north sides of the lake. An unobstructed view of the entire lake can be obtained from the dam on the east side. After checking the lake, park on the south side and take the hiking trail that winds its way through the cottonwood, elm, and willow woodlands on the west side of the lake. During the breeding season, you will find Warbling Vireos and Northern and Orchard Orioles.

200

*Sandsage
Prairie and
Short-grass
Prairie*

Located in Logan County in the heart of the short-grass prairie on the High Plains of western Kansas, Russell Springs offers birders several sites of interest. If you approach the town on K25 by traveling south over the 11.5 miles from the intersection with U.S. 40, it appears as an oasis in the valley of the Smoky Hill River. For this reason the town is a magnet for migrants. A good place to visit is Potter Park, just east of town. This park and campground with large stands of cottonwoods provides habitat for many Northern (Bullock's) Orioles in the spring and summer as well as for a variety of passerines during the spring and fall periods of passage. In the evening you can also expect to hear Common Poorwills.

Also check the K25 crossing of the Smoky Hill 0.6 mile south of town, since the riparian woodlands associated with the river, like all rivers of the High Plains, provide corridors for migrants that nest in the mountains to the west. Unfortunately, the continued drop in the water table due to irrigation has caused the

Although throwing himself skyward in an arching song-flight, the Cassin's Sparrow can be difficult to locate when quiet on the ground.

death of cottonwoods along these streams, especially along the Arkansas River.

A visit to the Logan Wildlife Management Area provides another opportunity to explore more riparian habitat as well as the associated prairie. At present, the lake is dry, but the Kansas Department of Wildlife and Parks plans to refill it. To reach this site, go 1.5 miles north on K25 from Russell Springs and turn left (west) on a gravel road. After 2. 5 miles you cross a cattle guard and enter the wildlife area. Bear to your left to reach the "lake" area.

SCOTT CITY, KANSAS

In the mid-1600s native Americans constructed El Cuartelejo Pueblo in the canyon of Ladder Creek; this site was excavated in 1889 and restored in 1970 as one of the attractions of Lake Scott State Park (permit required). Especially with the damming of spring-fed streams to form Lake Scott, this park is an important birding site on the High Plains. In summer the canyon slopes surrounding the lake are animated with scurrying Rock Wrens, while Mississippi Kites nest in the cottonwoods and can be seen floating overhead. Expect Yellow-breasted Chats during the breeding season. In the fall and winter you often see Prairie Falcons, and the lake attracts ducks and geese during migration. A few waterfowl tarry into the summer months, at least in small numbers. In the winter, Northern Shrikes have been regular on recent winter counts published by the Kansas Ornithological Society.

To reach the park go north on U.S. 83 from its intersection with K96 in Scott City for 10 miles and turn left on K95, which goes through the park and rejoins U.S. 83 about 5 miles farther north. After turning on K96, continue north for about 3 miles and turn left onto a hardtop road that circles the lake. A good place to stop soon after this turn-off is the Big Springs Nature Trail. The area is scenic and the trail short; and the springs attract many birds, particularly during migration and in the hot, dry days of summer. As you continue around the lake, you can stop to explore promising sites and scan the lake for waterfowl.

A worthwhile side trip on this tour, if back roads are dry, is to explore the Chalk Pyramids along the Smoky Hill River in Gove County, about 10 miles northeast of Lake Scott as the hawk flies. One mile north of the northern intersection of K96 with U.S. 83, the highway enters Logan County. Continue for 9 more miles and turn right (east) on a gravel road that becomes a graded dirt road in 2 miles. Follow this road for 4 miles to a "T" intersection. At this point turn right (south), and after about 3.5 miles you reach the eroded monuments laid down under Cretaceous seas. About 1.5 miles beyond this point the road crosses the Smoky Hill River, and after another 1.5 miles farther south a road to your right returns you west to U.S. 83 in 6.5 miles. Besides its

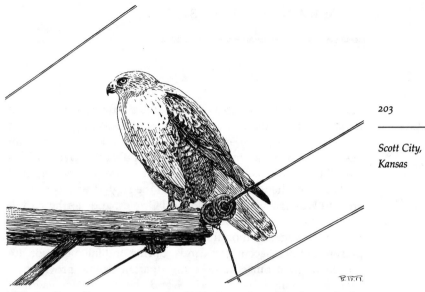

*Stop! Back up! That was not a red-tail! The Ferruginous Hawk nests in the
High Plains and drifts eastward from the short-grass prairie in winter.*

scenic value and geological interest, this loop takes you through
great raptor country. In fall, winter, and early spring you can
expect many Horned Larks and longspurs, but be sure to look
for the birds eating them. You can encounter most species of
falcons here sometime during the year. From fall to spring you
will find Red-tailed, Rough-legged, and Ferruginous Hawks as
well as Golden Eagles. In summer search for the nests of the
Ferruginous Hawks, frequently placed at the tops of inaccessible
chalk spires. Swainson's Hawks also return in summer to nest in
this area, and Prairie Falcons and Golden Eagles are summer
possibilities.

204

Sandsage Prairie and Short-grass Prairie

There are few public access areas in the northwestern corner of Kansas, but the 480-acre St. Francis Wildlife Management Area is one site that provides a birding opportunity in the riparian woodland along the south fork of the Republican River in Cheyenne County. In the breeding season the species you will find are typical of the woodland habitat of the High Plains: both Eastern and Western Kingbirds, Orchard Orioles, and Northern (Bullock's) Orioles are in the cottonwoods, and Northern Bobwhites feed in the vegetation on the ground. Western Meadowlarks are present in the adjacent grasslands. Spring and fall migration are especially good times because the riparian habitat provides an avenue for migrating passerines and the chance for vagrants from both east and west. Tennessee, Blackpoll, and Mac-Gillivray's Warblers have been seen here as well as Red-bellied Woodpecker, Least Flycatcher, Gray Catbird, Northern Waterthrush, Ovenbird, and Lazuli Bunting.

To reach the area, go west from St. Francis on u.s. 36; just before the bridge over the Republican River, turn left on an unmarked, hard-surfaced road that runs southwest. Continue for 3.5 miles, turn right onto a barely graded sand road, and drive for 0.4 mile to an open area where you can park. Just beyond the parking area to the west check a barrow pit pond for waterfowl during migration. South from the parking area a cottonwood woodland and open grasslands border the river.

I-70 TRANSECT

To help you become familiar with the birds of the area and allow escape from the sterile interstate as you travel this major east-west highway across the region of this guide, we identify a number of sites and briefly describe a few. The sequence is from east to west. If a return to I-70 is not given, go back the way you came. Several of the tours are loops that more or less parallel I-70. While they may be described from either an eastern or western entry, you can drive them in either direction.

Leave I-70 at the Blue Springs exit and proceed north on M7 for about 1 mile, then turn left, and go 0.5 mile to reach Burr Oak Woods. This 1,066-acre area includes a stand of mature, old growth chinquapin oak in the uplands and a rich woods of red and white oak, basswood, and walnut in the lowlands. The site is worth visiting during warbler migration and in the winter. Part of the site has been developed as a nature center.

Leave I-70 at exit 18 and follow Woods Chapel Road south to U.S. 40, jogging west briefly, and then south again to Lake Jacomo (see Lee's Summit MO). The easiest return is to take Woods Chapel Road west to I-470 and go north to I-70.

Leave I-70 at the West Lawrence exit of the Kansas Turnpike. Take U.S. 40 west to Clinton Lake or continue south on U.S. 59 (Iowa Street) to reach Baker Wetlands (see Lawrence KS).

Leave I-70 at exit 335 (Snokomo Road) and drive south through cultivated bottomlands where Dickcissels are abundant in the summer. In 4.2 miles the road climbs to upland prairie where you should expect to see the typical species of the tall-grass community. At 6.6 miles from I-70, stop opposite the Snokomo School and search the riparian vegetation on your right. About 2.5 miles from this point you come to a stop sign. Turn left, stopping at patches of dogwoods to listen for Bell's Vireos in the breeding season or to "swish" out mixed species flocks of sparrows in winter. In 2 miles from this turn you come to another stop sign at K4; turn left and follow this road, passing good prai-

rie on your left. Continue through Keene. At 3 miles since join-
ing ᴋ4, the highway bends left. Then in 0.5 mile turn left to return to ɪ-70 in 6.5 miles at exit 342. Alternatively, continue on ᴋ4
through Dover, reaching ɪ-70 in 16.3 miles on ᴋ4 at exit 353 after
passing through a mix of agricultural and suburban areas.

Take exit 313 and proceed south on ᴋ177 through well-managed
tall-grass prairie where you should expect Upland Sandpipers on
the fenceposts and Eastern Kingbirds, Eastern Meadowlarks,
and Dickcissels on the wires during the breeding season. If you
are fortunate, a Greater Prairie-chicken might fly across the road.
In the road cuts, Northern Rough-winged Swallows can be
found nesting in the limestone outcrops. About 2.5 miles from ɪ-
70 the road crosses a creek with a narrow fringe of riparian forest
where you might find Louisiana Waterthrushes and Summer
Tanagers.

At 15.2 miles from ɪ-70 turn left (east) on ᴋ4. Listen for Western Meadowlarks in the cultivated fields along the road. Then
turn left again in 1.5 miles on ᴋ180 into the town of Alta Vista.
Watch for Western Kingbirds in town. ᴋ180 ends, but continue
through town; bear right on the gravel road about 1.5 miles from
ᴋ4 and continue through excellent upland tall-grass prairie. At
4.8 miles from ᴋ4 park along the road just before crossing the
west branch of Mill Creek to investigate the cottonwoods along
the stream and the open stand of bur oak down the trail to your
right. If the acorn crop has been good, this is a good site for
wintering Red-headed Woodpeckers.

Continue for about 5.5 miles, just beyond the turn-off to Vol-
lard; stop and listen for Common Poorwills in the evening calling
from the rocky slope to your left. In winter, the brushy roadsides
along this part of the road are good for Harris' and American
Tree Sparrows, and you can expect Lark Sparrows during the
summer in the brushy overgrazed pastures. In another 2.5 miles,
it would be worthwhile to park again and explore the riparian
vegetation along both sides of the road. At 1.3 miles beyond,
good riparian vegetation runs along the right side of the road,
and in another 1.4 miles the dogwood on both sides of the road
usually has nesting Bell's Vireos.

In 2.5 miles from this stop you enter the town of Alma on
Third Street. At the first stop sign, turn left (north) on ᴋ99 (Missouri Street) and follow ᴋ99 through town and northward, returning to ɪ-70 at exit 328.

Take exit 303 and stop along the frontage road on the north side of the highway at the south gate to Konza Prairie Research Natural Area (do not block the gate). It is essential that you make prior arrangements with the Director of the Konza Prairie Research Natural Area (write, Division of Biology, Kansas State University, Manhattan KS 66506) before entering this preserve. When you do enter Konza Prairie, it is imperative that you stay on the trails and fireguards; do not walk across the open prairie since you will probably inadvertently interfere with on-going research. There are few birds on the prairie in winter, mainly raptors which you will have already identified from the highway; this excursion would offer nothing more than exercise at that time of year. But from early April through the end of October, park your car, climb over the gate, and then walk the graveled jeep trail as it curves to your left around the hill and then parallels the interstate. Soon the trail branches north to your right. Continue to follow this trail, but stop and listen. The watershed to your left is burned only every four years; in years when it is not burned, Henslow's Sparrows will be singing here from mid-April to July. In April and May you will also hear Greater Prairie-chickens displaying on the various "booming" grounds within hearing distance.

Bear to your right at the next trail junction. You should be seeing all the breeding species expected on the tall-grass prairie. To return to the south gate, turn right at the next fireguard and walk southeast. The watershed on your right is burned every odd year; the area on your left is burned every four years. As you come to the end of the ridge, you will be able to see how to follow the fireguards back to the gate. The stream below the pond with its thickets of prairie cordgrass is excellent for Sedge Wrens in August and September, and Le Conte's Sparrows in October. If you have more time, you can follow any of the fireguards to cover more of this excellent prairie, but just remember to stay on the fireguards.

Take exit 307 and proceed towards Manhattan on McDowell Creek Road (Riley Co. 901) for 4.7 miles to reach the main gate of the Konza Prairie Research Natural Area on your right (see Manhattan KS).

Take exit 295 and proceed south on u.s. 77 for 1.9 miles and turn right on the gravel road just south of the Smoky Hill River. This road goes along the edge of the floodplain with cultivated fields on the right and a mix of woody vegetation on the hillside to your left. In summer there will be few birds in the cultivated fields, but in the winter there will be mixed species flocks of both blackbirds and sparrows and often large concentrations of American Goldfinches and Pine Siskins in weedy fields. Concentrations of American Tree Sparrows in stands of uncut grain sorghum can be in the hundreds. During the breeding season, the hillside on the left will have nesting Bell's Vireos and Bewick's Wrens, while in some of the brushy pastures there will be Lark Sparrows.

At 1.6 miles from U.S. 77 you will come to a road that angles off to the right; take this to remain within the floodplain. In about 1 mile, the road skirts the edge of the bluffs along the Smoky Hill River. Soon you enter a forested creek valley. At 1.9 miles from where you turned right to stay within the floodplain there will be space to park by a gate on your right. Park here and spend some time exploring the edges of the woods as it borders the road. At sunset in the summer, this is a good place for Chuck-will's-widows and Barred Owls as well as Common Poorwills that can be heard calling from the upland prairies adjacent to this valley.

Continue on this road, and make a left turn in 0.7 mile. In 1 mile you come to a stop sign. Turn right here and continue for 1 mile; turn right for 0.5 mile and then turn left. In this area of cultivated uplands and grazed pastures, some fields contain stands of junipers. At 2 miles from this last corner, turn right and stop along the road in 0.1 mile to search the oaks on both sides of the road for Red-headed Woodpeckers. At 0.3 mile beyond this point the road turns left at the Smoky Hill River. At 0.8 mile from this last corner, stop the car where the road crosses a small stream and walk along the road in both directions. The old oxbow to the north of the road is often an excellent place from October to April for sparrows and blackbirds. You reach a stop sign at 1.2 miles beyond this last stopping place. Turn right on the hardtop, cross the Smoky Hill River, and continue straight through the town of Chapman to reach I-70 at exit 286 in 2.3 miles from the corner.

Leave I-70 at exit 233 and turn north towards the town of Westfall. This road goes through mixed farmlands with wheat, grain sorghum, and alfalfa as well as prairie pastures. In summer you can expect Western Meadowlarks, both Eastern and Western Kingbirds, and possibly Loggerhead Shrikes. In winter there will be Horned Larks, Lapland Longspurs, and several species of raptors, including Rough-legged Hawks and Northern Harriers. At 3.5 miles the road turns left (west) through some well-managed prairie and other overgrazed prairies. You should note the use of limestone for fenceposts in this area of few trees. At 10.3 miles from the corner, the road joins K14. Turn left and follow this highway to I-70 in 6.4 miles at exit 221.

Leave I-70 at exit 206 and go north on K232 to the Sylvan Park area at Wilson Lake (see Russell KS).

Leave I-70 on exit 145 and go south on K247 into the town of Ellis. At the traffic light turn left for 1 block, then turn right. At 5.8 miles from this corner turn left (east) onto a gravel road that continues east through a mix of good prairie, summer fallow, wheatfields, and grain sorghum. This route gives you a good sample of the birds of the mixed-grass prairie. In 12 miles you come to a stop sign where the road joins bypass U.S. 40 in Hays. Turn right and continue for 0.5 mile to a blinker light where you should turn left into Frontier Park. On the other side of the highway you should also explore the Fort Hays Experiment Station plantings for birds. Both sites are especially good during passerine migration since these wooded habitats form an island in the plains that frequently attracts a variety of warblers, included vagrant eastern species. One mile beyond the blinker light the bypass joins U.S. 183. Turn left and continue north on Vine Street to I-70 in 2.5 miles at exit 159.

It's more than 10 miles south from the interstate to reach Cedar Bluff Reservoir, but this loop, starting from either exit 127 at WaKeeney or exit 135 at Ogallah, is probably worth following (see WaKeeney KS).

At exit 107 go north on K212 into Quinter to visit the Sheridan Wildlife Area (see Quinter KS).

Leave I-70 at Goodland on exit 17 and take K27 south for 6.5 miles. Then turn right and go 2 miles west; then turn left (south) and continue for 3 more miles. At this point turn right into the Sherman County State Fishing Lake and Wildlife Management Area. In 1.3 miles you reach the dam of the lake, which may or may not have water. A road across the dam provides access to the west side. There are good riparian cottonwoods and willows below the dam with several active springs. This area is especially good for migrant passerines. In summer there are Orchard and Northern (Bullock's) Orioles, Eastern and Western Kingbirds, Dickcissels, and Red-winged Blackbirds.

If you return to the entrance of the wildlife area, cross over to the Sherman County Park with a lake that has water and does attract waterfowl during migration. The lake is narrow, and the area around the lake is mowed. However, a few cottonwood groves do attract passerines.

CHECKLIST OF THE BIRDS OF
KANSAS AND WESTERN MISSOURI

LOONS, GREBES
Red-throated Loon
Pacific Loon
Common Loon
Pied-billed Grebe
Horned Grebe
Red-necked Grebe
Eared Grebe
Western Grebe
Clark's Grebe

PELICANS
White Pelican
Brown Pelican

CORMORANTS, ANHINGA
Double-crested Cormorant
Olivaceous Cormorant
Anhinga

FRIGATEBIRD
Magnificent Frigatebird

HERONS
American Bittern
Least Bittern
Great Blue Heron
Great Egret
Snowy Egret
Little Blue Heron
Tricolored Heron
Cattle Egret
Green-backed Heron
Black-crowned Night-heron
Yellow-crowned Night-heron

IBIS, STORK
White Ibis
White-faced Ibis

Roseate Spoonbill
Wood Stork

FLAMINGO
Greater Flamingo

WHISTLING-DUCKS
Fulvous Whistling-duck
Black-bellied Whistling-duck

SWANS
Tundra Swan
Trumpeter Swan

GEESE
Greater White-fronted Goose
Snow Goose
Ross' Goose
Brant
Canada Goose

DUCKS
Wood Duck
Green-winged Teal
American Black Duck
Mottled Duck
Mallard
Northern Pintail
Garganey
Blue-winged Teal
Cinnamon Teal
Northern Shoveler
Gadwall
Eurasian Wigeon
American Wigeon
Canvasback
Redhead
Ring-necked Duck
Greater Scaup

211
—————

Checklist of the
Birds of the
Region

Lesser Scaup
Common Eider
King Eider
Oldsquaw
Black Scoter
Surf Scoter
White-winged Scoter
Common Goldeneye
Bufflehead
Hooded Merganser
Common Merganser
Red-breasted Merganser
Ruddy Duck

VULTURES
Black Vulture
Turkey Vulture

KITES
American Swallow-tailed Kite
Black-shouldered Kite
Mississippi Kite

HAWKS, EAGLES
Osprey
Bald Eagle
Northern Harrier
Sharp-shinned Hawk
Cooper's Hawk
Northern Goshawk
Harris' Hawk
Red-shouldered Hawk
Broad-winged Hawk
Swainson's Hawk
Red-tailed Hawk
Ferruginous Hawk
Rough-legged Hawk
Golden Eagle

FALCONS
American Kestrel
Merlin
Peregrine Falcon
Gyrfalcon
Prairie Falcon

212

Checklist of the
Birds of the
Region

PHEASANT
Ring-necked Pheasant

PRAIRIE CHICKENS, GROUSE
Ruffed Grouse
Greater Prairie-chicken
Lesser Prairie-chicken
Sharp-tailed Grouse

TURKEY
Wild Turkey

QUAILS
Northern Bobwhite
Scaled Quail

RAILS AND GALLINULES
Yellow Rail
Black Rail
King Rail
Virginia Rail
Sora
Purple Gallinule
Common Moorhen
American Coot

CRANES
Sandhill Crane
Whooping Crane

PLOVERS
Black-bellied Plover
Lesser Golden Plover
Snowy Plover
Semipalmated Plover
Piping Plover
Killdeer
Mountain Plover

STILTS AND AVOCETS
Black-necked Stilt
American Avocet

SANDPIPERS
Greater Yellowlegs
Lesser Yellowlegs
Solitary Sandpiper

Willet
Spotted Sandpiper
Upland Sandpiper
Eskimo Curlew
Whimbrel
Long-billed Curlew
Hudsonian Godwit
Marbled Godwit
Ruddy Turnstone
Red Knot
Sanderling
Semipalmated Sandpiper
Western Sandpiper
Least Sandpiper
White-rumped Sandpiper
Baird's Sandpiper
Pectoral Sandpiper
Dunlin
Curlew Sandpiper
Stilt Sandpiper
Buff-breasted Sandpiper
Ruff
Short-billed Dowitcher
Long-billed Dowitcher
Common Snipe
American Woodcock

PHALAROPES
Wilson's Phalarope
Red-necked Phalarope
Red Phalarope

JAEGERS
Pomarine Jaeger
Parasitic Jaeger
Long-tailed Jaeger

GULLS
Laughing Gull
Franklin's Gull
Little Gull
Bonaparte's Gull
Ring-billed Gull
California Gull

Herring Gull
Thayer's Gull
Glaucous Gull
Black-legged Kittiwake
Sabine's Gull

TERNS
Caspian Tern
Common Tern
Forster's Tern
Least Tern
Black Tern

SKIMMER
Black Skimmer

PIGEONS
Rock Dove
Band-tailed Pigeon

DOVES
Mourning Dove
Inca Dove
Common Ground Dove

CUCKOOS
Black-billed Cuckoo
Yellow-billed Cuckoo
Greater Roadrunner
Groove-billed Ani

OWLS
Common Barn-owl
Eastern Screech-owl
Western Screech-owl
Great Horned Owl
Snowy Owl
Burrowing Owl
Barred Owl
Long-eared Owl
Short-eared Owl
Northern Saw-whet Owl

GOATSUCKERS
Common Nighthawk
Common Poorwill

Checklist of the
Birds of the
Region

Chuck-will's-widow
Whip-poor-will

SWIFTS
Chimney Swift
White-throated Swift

214

Checklist of the
Birds of the
Region

HUMMINGBIRDS
Magnificent Hummingbird
Ruby-throated Hummingbird
Black-chinned Hummingbird
Calliope Hummingbird
Broad-tailed Hummingbird
Rufous Hummingbird

KINGFISHER
Belted Kingfisher

WOODPECKERS
Lewis' Woodpecker
Red-headed Woodpecker
Red-bellied Woodpecker
Yellow-bellied Sapsucker
Williamson's Sapsucker
Ladder-backed Woodpecker
Downy Woodpecker
Hairy Woodpecker
Northern Flicker
Pileated Woodpecker

FLYCATCHERS
Olive-sided Flycatcher
Western Wood-pewee
Eastern Wood-pewee
Yellow-bellied Flycatcher
Acadian Flycatcher
Alder Flycatcher
Willow Flycatcher
Least Flycatcher
Hammond's Flycatcher
Dusky Flycatcher
Gray Flycatcher
Western Flycatcher
Eastern Phoebe

Say's Phoebe
Vermilion Flycatcher
Ash-throated Flycatcher
Great Crested Flycatcher
Cassin's Kingbird
Western Kingbird
Eastern Kingbird
Scissor-tailed Flycatcher

LARK
Horned Lark

SWALLOWS
Purple Martin
Tree Swallow
Violet-green Swallow
Northern Rough-winged Swallow
Bank Swallow
Cliff Swallow
Barn Swallow

JAYS, MAGPIES, CROWS
Steller's Jay
Blue Jay
Scrub Jay
Gray-breasted Jay
Pinyon Jay
Clark's Nutcracker
Black-billed Magpie
American Crow
Chihuahuan Raven
Common Raven

CHICKADEES, TITMOUSE
Black-capped Chickadee
Carolina Chickadee
Mountain Chickadee
Tufted Titmouse

BUSHTIT
Bushtit

NUTHATCHES
Red-breasted Nuthatch

White-breasted Nuthatch
Pygmy Nuthatch

CREEPER
Brown Creeper

WRENS
Rock Wren
Carolina Wren
Bewick's Wren
House Wren
Winter Wren
Sedge Wren
Marsh Wren

KINGLETS
Golden-crowned Kinglet
Ruby-crowned Kinglet

GNATCATCHER
Blue-gray Gnatcatcher

THRUSHES
Eastern Bluebird
Mountain Bluebird
Townsend's Solitaire
Veery
Gray-cheeked Thrush
Swainson's Thrush
Hermit Thrush
Wood Thrush
American Robin
Varied Thrush

THRASHERS
Gray Catbird
Northern Mockingbird
Sage Thrasher
Brown Thrasher
Curve-billed Thrasher

PIPITS
Water Pipit
Sprague's Pipit

WAXWINGS
Bohemian Waxwing
Cedar Waxwing

SHRIKES
Northern Shrike
Loggerhead Shrike

STARLING
European Starling

VIREOS
White-eyed Vireo
Bell's Vireo
Black-capped Vireo
Solitary Vireo
Yellow-throated Vireo
Warbling Vireo
Philadelphia Vireo
Red-eyed Vireo

WARBLERS
Blue-winged Warbler
Golden-winged Warbler
Tennessee Warbler
Orange-crowned Warbler
Nashville Warbler
Virginia's Warbler
Northern Parula
Yellow Warbler
Chestnut-sided Warbler
Magnolia Warbler
Cape May Warbler
Black-throated Blue Warbler
Yellow-rumped Warbler
Black-throated Gray Warbler
Townsend's Warbler
Hermit Warbler
Black-throated Green Warbler
Blackburnian Warbler
Yellow-throated Warbler
Pine Warbler
Prairie Warbler

Checklist of the
Birds of the
Region

Palm Warbler
Bay-breasted Warbler
Blackpoll Warbler
Cerulean Warbler
Black-and-white Warbler
American Redstart
Prothonotary Warbler
Worm-eating Warbler
Swainson's Warbler
Ovenbird
Northern Waterthrush
Louisiana Waterthrush
Kentucky Warbler
Connecticut Warbler
Mourning Warbler
MacGillivray's Warbler
Common Yellowthroat
Hooded Warbler
Wilson's Warbler
Canada Warbler
Yellow-breasted Chat

TANAGERS
Summer Tanager
Scarlet Tanager
Western Tanager

GROSBEAKS, BUNTINGS
Northern Cardinal
Rose-breasted Grosbeak
Black-headed Grosbeak
Blue Grosbeak
Lazuli Bunting
Indigo Bunting
Painted Bunting
Dickcissel

SPARROWS
Green-tailed Towhee
Rufous-sided Towhee
Brown Towhee
Bachman's Sparrow
Cassin's Sparrow
Rufous-crowned Sparrow

American Tree Sparrow
Chipping Sparrow
Clay-colored Sparrow
Brewer's Sparrow
Field Sparrow
Vesper Sparrow
Lark Sparrow
Black-throated Sparrow
Sage Sparrow
Lark Bunting
Savannah Sparrow
Baird's Sparrow
Grasshopper Sparrow
Henslow's Sparrow
Le Conte's Sparrow
Sharp-tailed Sparrow
Fox Sparrow
Song Sparrow
Lincoln's Sparrow
Swamp Sparrow
White-throated Sparrow
Golden-crowned Sparrow
White-crowned Sparrow
Harris' Sparrow
Dark-eyed Junco
McCown's Longspur
Lapland Longspur
Smith's Longspur
Chestnut-collared Longspur
Snow Bunting

BLACKBIRDS, ORIOLES
Bobolink
Red-winged Blackbird
Eastern Meadowlark
Western Meadowlark
Yellow-headed Blackbird
Rusty Blackbird
Brewer's Blackbird
Great-tailed Grackle
Common Grackle
Brown-headed Cowbird
Orchard Oriole

216

Checklist of the
Birds of the
Region

Northern Oriole
Scott's Oriole

FINCHES
Pine Grosbeak
Purple Finch
Cassin's Finch
House Finch
Red Crossbill

White-winged Crossbill
Common Redpoll
Pine Siskin
Lesser Goldfinch
American Goldfinch
Evening Grosbeak

WEAVER FINCH
House Sparrow

*Checklist of the
Birds of the
Region*

SPECIALTY SPECIES

Additional notes for species with restricted habitat preferences and/
or ranges within the area and, if appropriate, the location of most
probable occurrence.

Common Loon. Present on all large reservoirs throughout the
region, but especially east of the mixed-grass prairie. Larger
impoundments around Kansas City especially good.
Horned Grebe. Less probable west of the tall-grass prairie.
Eared Grebe. During migration on lakes and reservoirs throughout
the area, but especially west of the oak-hickory and Ozark
forests. During the breeding season, can be expected at Quivira
National Wildlife Refuge and at Cheyenne Bottoms.
Western Grebe. Most probable during fall migration on reservoirs
west of the tall-grass prairie like Cedar Bluff and Kirwin National
Wildlife Refuge.
Clark's Grebe. Probable in the same areas suggested for the Western
Grebe.
Double-crested Cormorant. Breeds at Kirwin National Wildlife
Refuge.
Least Bittern. Most easily observed in cattail marshes throughout
the area from mid-June into July when adults make numerous
flights while feeding young.
White-faced Ibis. Nesting populations present at Cheyenne Bottoms
and Quivira National Wildlife Refuge. When water levels ideal,
species common at these sites.
Mottled Duck. A small, isolated, disjunct nesting population
present at Cheyenne Bottoms. Its status unclear.
Cinnamon Teal. A regular low density transient in appropriate
habitat from the mixed-grass prairie westward. Not to be
expected in Missouri.
Mississippi Kite. Regular from May through September in the
southern mixed-grass prairie, sand prairie, cedar hills prairie,
sandsage prairie, and southern short-grass plains. Check mature
windbreak plantings and towns.
Ferruginous Hawk. During the summer occurs in short-grass prairie
of the High Plains, especially in the dissected chalk bluff areas in

southwestern Gove County, Kansas. In winter occurs regularly
from the mixed-grass prairie westward.

Golden Eagle. To be expected in the winter in the short-grass prairie.
Rare in northwest Missouri during fall migration and early
winter.

Merlin. Besides occurring as a migrant throughout the region, a
fairly common resident from December through February in
southwestern Kansas in some years. Look for it in the Cimarron
National Grasslands.

Prairie Falcon. Regular in the winter as far east as the tall-grass
prairie. Look for it in upland prairie sites west of the tall-grass
prairie where Horned Larks and longspurs are abundant. In the
tall-grass prairie area most probable in cultivated areas where
uncut grain sorghum attracts flocks of sparrows and blackbirds.
In summer possibly present at low densities west of the mixed-
grass prairie.

Greater Prairie-chicken. Indicator species of well-managed tall-grass
prairie. Most easily discovered from March through May by
listening for leks of displaying males. Common in the Flint Hills
Upland where these display ("booming") grounds are located on
the thinner soils of claypan sites on the ridges.

Lesser Prairie-chicken. Most regular in the Cimarron National
Grasslands.

Scaled Quail. To be seen all year in the Cimarron National
Grasslands. Watch for in sandsage prairie and in and around
farm yards and discarded farm machinery.

Black Rail. Occurs in the wet meadow at Quivira National Wildlife
Refuge.

Sandhill Crane. Common around reservoirs and wetlands west of
the tall-grass prairie from mid-March to mid-April and
throughout October.

Whooping Crane. Of fairly regular occurrence from late October
through early November in central Kansas. Both Cheyenne
Bottoms and Quivira National Wildlife Refuge host this
endangered species from time to time. Check with the refuge
managers.

Snowy Plover. Look on saline flats at Quivira National Wildlife
Refuge.

Black-necked Stilt. Breeds in marsh areas at Quivira National
Wildlife Refuge.

Buff-breasted Sandpiper. Possible in drier fields associated with
prairie dog towns around Cheyenne Bottoms and dried up

portions of the peripheral pools at Squaw Creek National Wildlife Refuge.

Least Tern. From mid-May until late August can be seen around saline marshes at Quivira National Wildlife Refuge. Also a possibility where the Barber–Comanche counties tour (Medicine Lodge KS) comes close to the Salt Fork of the Arkansas River.

Burrowing Owl. Present from early April through September in prairie dog towns from the sand prairie westward.

Common Poorwill. Readily heard throughout the breeding season beginning in mid-April from the Flint Hills westward. Associated with rock outcrops and ledges in grassland communities.

Ladder-backed Woodpecker. Reliably found only in larger stands of cottonwood along the Cimarron River in the Cimarron National Grasslands. Fall and winter seem best seasons.

Acadian Flycatcher. Breeds in riparian forests and shaded ravines near water in upland forests in the oak-hickory and Ozark forest communities.

Willow Flycatcher. Present as a breeding species in wet oldfield habitats east of the tall-grass prairie.

Say's Phoebe. Present from the mixed-grass prairie westward.

Ash-throated Flycatcher. Watch along the Cimarron River in May and September on the Cimarron National Grasslands.

Cassin's Kingbird. Possible breeding species in the sandsage prairie area (Cimarron National Grasslands) and cedar hills prairie (Barber–Comanche counties tour).

Scissor-tailed Flycatcher. Most probable from mid-April until October in the southern half of tall-grass prairie region and sand prairie area, but regularly occurs at the same latitudes across the forest-prairie mosaic.

Black-billed Magpie. To be expected as a permanent resident from the mixed-grass and sand prairies westward.

Chihuahuan Raven. Look all year on the Cimarron National Grasslands.

Mountain Chickadee. Occasionally found in winter at Elkhart KS.

Rock Wren. Present as a breeding species from April until October in rock outcrop habitats from the mixed-grass prairie westward.

Carolina Wren. Permanent resident in riparian habitats in the Ozark forest, oak-hickory forest, and the forest-prairie mosaic.

Bewick's Wren. Most easily found by investigating shrub thickets in the tall-grass and sand prairies.

Sedge Wren. Present from May to October as a breeding species but with a peculiar seasonality. In May found in wet meadow and oldfield habitats in the areas of the oak-hickory and forest-prairie mosaic regions. Later (July to September) appears at Taberville Prairie in Missouri as well farther west in tall-grass prairie (for example, in the prairie cordgrass swales at the Konza Prairie Research Natural Area).

Marsh Wren. During migration found in cattail and smartweed marshes in the eastern part of the region. Nests only sparingly (for example, Cheyenne Bottoms). Regular in cattail marshes during the winter in the mixed-grass prairie westward.

Mountain Bluebird. Present in winter from the mixed-grass prairie westward, especially in the southern half of the region.

Townsend's Solitaire. Winter resident as a cedar thicket obligate. Can be regularly expected in such habitat as far east as the tall-grass prairie.

Wood Thrush. Summer resident from mid-April to late September throughout the Ozark forest, oak-hickory forest, forest-prairie mosaic, and in localized sites west to tall-grass prairie.

Sage Thrasher. Best chance in the fall at the Cimarron National Grasslands.

Curve-billed Thrasher. Throughout the sandsage prairie area found during winter in towns and associated with isolated cholla cactus in summer.

Northern Shrike. Regular during winter in the mixed-grass prairie and short-grass prairie at such sites as Cedar Bluff Reservoir and Scott Lake State Park.

White-eyed Vireo. From late April until early October throughout the Ozark forest, oak-hickory forest, and forest-prairie mosaic regions, found in second-growth riparian forests with well-developed understory.

Bell's Vireo. A bird of thickets from edge habitats in the oak-hickory forest in the eastern part of the region west to woody thickets (for example, dogwood, wild plum) associated with the tall-grass, mixed-grass, and sand prairie.

Yellow-throated Vireo. Occurs as breeding species within the Ozark forest, oak-hickory forest, and forest-prairie mosaic regions where the deciduous trees are tall and the canopy of the forest is at least partially open.

Blue-winged Warbler. Present in mature oldfield and forest edge communities in the Ozark forest and oak-hickory areas from late April until September.

Northern Parula. Expected as a breeding bird of riparian forests in the Ozark forest, oak-hickory forest, forest-prairie mosaic, and tall-grass prairie regions.

Yellow-throated Warbler. Occurs as breeding species in riparian forests in the Ozark Plateau (Schermerhorn Park) and possibly in bottomland habitats farther west in the forest-prairie mosaic.

Pine Warbler. Can be found in pine stands within the Ozark Plateau.

Prairie Warbler. Nests in forest edge and oldfield communities within the Ozark forest region.

Cerulean Warbler. A breeding bird in mature riparian forests in the Ozark forest, oak-hickory, and forest-prairie mosaic regions.

Prothonotary Warbler. A nesting species in bottomland riparian forests from the oak-hickory forest and Ozark forest through the forest-prairie mosaic to the edge of the tall-grass prairie region.

Worm-eating Warbler. A breeding species on moist slopes of upland deciduous forest in the Ozark forest, oak-hickory forest, and forest-prairie mosaic.

Ovenbird. Present as a nesting species from late April through September in upland forests within the Ozark forest, oak-hickory forest, and forest-prairie mosaic regions.

Louisiana Waterthrush. Present from the end of March until September in forested creek valleys close to water from the eastern edge of the region west to the gallery forests in the tall-grass prairie.

Kentucky Warbler. Like preceding species, can be found from May until September west to the tall-grass prairie. Expected in forested riparian habitats with a well-developed understory.

Macgillivray's Warbler. Although this western warbler can turn up in any small island of appropriate habitat throughout the short-grass plains during migration, quite regular in May and September in the brushy vegetation at Point of Rocks on the Cimarron National Grasslands tour.

Hooded Warbler. Best chance of seeing at the western fringe of its breeding range in overgrown, second-growth habitats at Roaring River State Park and adjacent national forest land.

Summer Tanager. Present as a summer resident throughout the Ozark forest, oak-hickory forest, forest-prairie mosaic, and as far west as the gallery forests of the tall-grass prairie area. Observed more frequently in upland forests, but also occurs in riparian deciduous forest.

Scarlet Tanager. Summer distribution of this species more restricted to the eastern part of the region, primarily present in the Ozark forest and oak-hickory forest communities. Prefers mature riparian or upland forest stands with intermediate to large-sized oaks as conspicuous members of the plant community.

Western Tanager. A low density migrant during September along the Cimarron River on the Cimarron National Grasslands.

Rose-breasted Grosbeak. Present from late April until mid-September as a breeding species in the same areas as the Summer Tanager, but more frequently observed in open, mature bottomland forests than in similarly open, mature upland stands. Also expected in riparian forests farther west in the mixed-grass prairie and sand prairie regions.

Black-headed Grosbeak. A breeding species in riparian woodlands from the short-grass plains east to the sand prairie and mixed-grass prairies.

Blue Grosbeak. Present in mature oldfield and forest edge communities as well as more open deciduous forests from late April through late August from the eastern edge of the region west to the mixed-grass prairie and sand prairie areas.

Painted Bunting. Summer resident present in low numbers in mature oldfield and edge communities in the Ozark forest and southern forest-prairie mosaic regions west across the southern part of the tall-grass prairie to the cedar hills prairie.

Green-tailed Towhee. Possible with careful searching in edge habitats during migration on the Cimarron National Grasslands tour.

Brown Towhee. Expected at low densities at the Cimarron National Grasslands, especially at Point of Rocks.

Bachman's Sparrow. Possible in association with glades at Table Rock Lake.

Cassin's Sparrow. Present in the short-grass prairie of the High Plains from May through August, but most easily found during the early summer because of its "skylarking" song display.

Rufous-crowned Sparrow. Most probable at Point of Rocks at the Cimarron National Grasslands.

Brewer's Sparrow. Arrives in late April to breed in sandsage prairie and short-grass prairie that has a well-developed stand of sagebrush. Best possibility for finding on the Cimarron National Grasslands tour by searching appropriate habitat, particularly around Wilburton KS.

Lark Bunting. Short-grass prairie counterpart of the Dickcissel. Found in oldfield and brushy prairie sites throughout the High Plains. Most readily found along roadsides anywhere in this area.

Henslow's Sparrow. Arrives in mid-April and remains until late September. Like many grassland birds most easily discovered during the season when most actively singing, May through the first week of July. Restricted to tall-grass prairie habitat with well-developed patches of standing dead vegetation and dense litter; hence does not occur in prairies burned that spring or prairies even moderately grazed the previous year. Only regular sites are the Konza Prairie Research Natural Area and Taberville Prairie.

Le Conte's Sparrow. Migrant most easily found during October throughout the tall-grass and sand prairie areas in grassland habitats with shrubby vegetation.

Swamp Sparrow. Common transient and winter resident in the oak-hickory and forest-prairie mosaic areas. Can also be expected west into the tall-grass prairie community in wet oldfield habitats.

Harris' Sparrow. Most easily found from October through March from the mixed-grass prairie east into Missouri. Especially favorable habitats are multiflora rose hedges and windbreak plantings.

McCown's Longspur. Search all flocks of longspurs in the western half of Kansas; best chances in migration and winter at the Cimarron National Grasslands.

Smith's Longspur. Best chance of finding in mowed prairie in the vicinity of Lyon County State Fishing Lake from October through April. Occasionally found in November and December on the Taberville Prairie in Missouri.

Chestnut-collared Longspur. Check carefully winter flocks of Lapland Longspurs from the mixed-grass prairie west to the short-grass plains. Apparently regular at Cimarron National Grasslands and in the vicinity of Scott Lake State Park.

Bobolink. Can be found as a spring transient during May east from the forest-prairie mosaic. Also disjunct breeding population at the Quivira National Wildlife Refuge in the sand prairie area. Occasionally found in summer in the vicinity of Smithville Lake and fairly common fall migrant in western Missouri.

Yellow-headed Blackbird. Present in deep-water cattail marshes from early April until October in the mixed-grass and sand prairie areas.

Great-tailed Grackle. Breeds most regularly throughout the mixed-grass and sand prairie areas; more regular in the southern part of this region.

House Finch. Found all year in mixed-grass and sand prairie areas and westward. Most easily seen in towns.

BIBLIOGRAPHY

Branan, W. V., and H. C. Burdick. 1981. Bird species composition in a Missouri park, 1916 vs 1973. *Kansas Ornithological Society Bulletin* 32: 41–45.

Buchanan, R., ed. 1984. *Kansas Geology.* Lawrence: University Press of Kansas.

Clawson, Richard L. 1982. *The status, distribution, and habitat preferences of the birds of Missouri.* Terrestrial Series. No. 11. Jefferson City: Missouri Department of Conservation.

Ely, Charles A. 1971. *A history and distributional list of Ellis County, Kansas birds.* Fort Hays Studies—New Series. Science Series No. 9. Hays KS: Fort Hays State University.

Ernsting, G. W. 1984. Nesting distribution in Kansas of selected colonial nesting herons in 1982 and 1983. Master's thesis, Fort Hays State University, Hays KS.

Flora, S. D. 1948. *Climate of Kansas.* Report. Topeka: Kansas State Board of Agriculture, 67.

Johnston, Richard F. 1964. *The breeding birds of Kansas.* University of Kansas Publication Museum of Natural History 12: 575–655.

———. 1965. *A directory to the birds of Kansas.* University of Kansas Museum of Natural History Miscellaneous Publication 41: 1–67.

Kahl, R. B., T. S. Baskett, J. A. Ellis, and J. N. Burroughs. 1985. *Characteristics of summer habitats of selected nongame birds in Missouri.* Agricultural Experiment Station Research Bulletin No. 1056. Columbia: University of Missouri.

Kansas Ornithological Society. 1982. Check List: Birds of Kansas.

Kuchler, A. W. 1974. A new vegetation map of Kansas. *Ecology* 55: 586–604.

Rafferty, M. D. 1983. *Missouri, a Geography.* Boulder CO: Westview Press.

Schoewe, W. H. 1949. The geography of Kansas. Part II. Physical geography. *Transactions of the Kansas Academy of Science* 52: 261–333.

Skinner, R. M., T. S. Baskett, and M. D. Blenden. 1984. *Bird habitats on Missouri prairies.* Terrestrial Series No. 14. Jefferson City: Missouri Department of Conservation.

Steyermark, J. A. 1963. *Flora of Missouri.* Ames: Iowa State University Press.

Thom, R. H., and G. Iffrig. 1985. *Directory of Missouri Natural Areas.* Missouri Natural Areas Committee. Jefferson City: Missouri Department of Conservation.

Thorton, K. W. 1984. *Regional Comparisons of Lakes and Reservoirs: Geology, Climatology, and Morphology.* Lakes and Reservoir Management. EPA 440/5-84-001. Pp. 261–65. Washington, DC: Government Printing Office.

INDEX TO BIRD NAMES

230

Longspur, 10, 59, 176, 184, 189, 190, 203, 220
   Chestnut-collared, 142, 190, 191, 197, 225
   Lapland, 109, 142, 189, 190, 209, 225
   McCown's, 190, 191, 197, 225
   Smith's, 112, 225
Loon, Common, 31, 116, 118, 131, 219

Magpie, Black-billed, 6, 136, 167, 172, 179, 184, 190, 221
Mallard, 45, 91, 116, 150, 163, 172, 177, 180
Martin, Purple, 60
Meadowlark, Eastern, 2, 7, 40, 50, 85, 109, 111, 117, 119, 206
   Western, 8, 50, 85, 117, 165, 177, 204, 206, 208
Merganser, Common, 46, 66, 77, 116, 172, 180
   Hooded, 46, 66, 77, 180
   Red-breasted, 77
Merlin, 189, 190, 198, 220
Mockingbird, Northern, 29, 38, 149, 177
Moorhen, Common, 60

Nighthawk, Common, 7, 109
Night-heron, Black-crowned, 84, 86, 194
   Yellow-crowned, 80, 84, 86, 142
Nuthatch, Red-breasted, 66, 144
   White-breasted, 21, 28, 31, 45, 46, 51, 79, 85, 129, 135

Oldsquaw, 66, 116, 131
Oriole, Baltimore, 1, 93, 95
   Bullock's, 1, 6, 164, 185, 190, 200, 204, 210
   Northern, 38, 128, 129, 176, 199
   Orchard, 6, 32, 38, 76, 95, 135, 139, 164, 172, 176, 177, 190, 197, 199, 204, 210
Osprey, 55, 63, 81, 118

Ovenbird, 5, 22, 26, 30, 50, 76, 82, 204, 223
Owl, Barred, 22, 28, 77, 79, 82, 84, 100, 155, 208
   Burrowing, 7, 139, 141, 157, 172, 221
   Great Horned, 22, 28, 29, 66, 84, 100, 139, 177, 190
   Long-eared, 65, 66, 101, 112, 114, 184
   Northern Saw-whet, 65, 100, 114
   Short-eared, 37, 58, 61, 85, 101, 112, 140, 189

Parula, Northern, 5, 6, 22, 26, 45, 50, 58, 66, 70, 79, 80, 82, 85, 86, 91, 94, 222
Pelican, American White, 53, 60, 81, 118, 119, 177, 182, 196
Phalarope, Wilson's, 60, 100, 137, 152, 172, 197
Phoebe, Eastern, 25, 45, 85, 155
   Say's, 2, 7, 155, 178, 221
Pintail, Northern, 10, 86, 91, 150, 172, 177
Pipit, Sprague's, 37
Plover, Black-bellied, 118
   Lesser Golden, 55, 81
   Mountain, 8
   Semipalmated, 83
   Snowy, 127, 152, 220
Poorwill, Common, 2, 7, 109, 110, 120, 190, 200, 206, 208, 221
Prairie-chicken, Greater, 1, 7, 37, 109, 110, 112, 119, 120, 191, 206, 207, 220
   Lesser, 2, 8, 136, 155, 191, 194, 220

Quail, Scaled, 2, 8, 190, 191, 194, 220

Rail, Black, 60, 152, 220
   King, 60, 100, 137, 140, 152
   Virginia, 80, 100, 140, 152

INDEX TO PLACE NAMES

Numbers in italics refer to maps.

244

Index
to Place
Names